Breaking Away from the Textbook

Creative Ways to Teach World History

Ron H. Pahl

Volume 2
The Enlightenment through the 20th Century

scarecrow
education

The Scarecrow Press, Inc.
A Scarecrow Education Book
Lanham, Maryland, and London
2002

SCARECROW PRESS, INC.
SCARECROW EDUCATION

Published in the United States of America
by Scarecrow Press, Inc.
4720 Boston Way
Lanham, Maryland 20706
www.scarecrowpress.com

4 Pleydell Gardens, Folkestone
Kent CT20 2 DN, England

British Library Cataloguing in Publication Information Available

Library of Congress Cataloging-in-Publication Data

Pahl, Ron H., 1943–
    Breaking away from the textbook : creative ways to teach
world history / Ron H. Pahl.
        p. cm. — (A Scarecrow education book)
    Includes bibliography.
    Contents: v. 1. Prehistory to 1600 — v. 2. The
enlightenment through the twentieth century.
    ISBN 0-8108-3760-9 (alk. paper)
        1. History—Study and teaching. I. Title.
D16.2 .P24 2002   2001020970
907'.1—dc21
v. 1 ISBN 0-8108-3759-5
set   ISBN 0-8108-3761-7

Contents

List of Illustrations

Acknowledgments

This work could not have been accomplished without the unwavering support and commitment of my wife, Jarvis, and my grown children, Mothusi and Leloba. The others whose suggestions greatly improved the quality of *Breaking Away from the Textbook: Creative Ways to Teach World History* are Dick and Judy Kraft, Nelson and JoAnne Woodard, Bill Lacey, John Bovberg, and Ron Evans. Also not to be forgotten are the many teachers and student teachers who tested, commented on, and corrected items in the Thematic Lesson Pacs in these volumes.

Introduction

The purpose of the series *Breaking Away from the Textbook: Creative Ways to Teach World History* is simple—to make the teaching and learning of world history a powerful and enjoyable experience in the classroom. All too often, our students tell us that world history is the most boring subject they have at school. This series of Thematic Lesson Pacs hopes to change this image of world history for both teachers and students. From the size of this volume, you can tell it is not a comprehensive world history guide, nor is it a text heavy into theory. Instead, this book focuses on the following:

- A wide variety of active teaching ideas for world history
- A large number of ideas on how to get students excited about world history
- How-to-do-it brainstorms for teachers who know they need help
- Neat ways to have students grapple with the major problems and issues humanity has faced throughout history
- Innovative ways to help students see the relevance of major people, events, and ideas of the past to our lives today

Simply put, the purpose of the book is to make world history fun. Teachers and students can select all or parts of the world history Thematic Lesson Pacs (TLPs) in this volume to enhance their study of a particular historical person, event, or idea. Personal choice from a wide variety of different activities is a key feature of the *Breaking Away from the Textbook* series.

These volumes, however, are not for everyone. Those who should not use these volumes are the following:

- Teachers who enjoy boring their students with endless lectures
- Teachers who believe that their students must memorize every name and date in their textbook
- Teachers who demand a quiet classroom with students reading their textbook, filling in the blanks of worksheets, and answering the questions at the end of the chapter

A word of caution, however, should also be made. Reading the textbook is important. The active learning strategies presented in this book are not meant to discourage reading. Rather, these strategies are designed to get students turned on to the ideas and problems humans have faced throughout history. Students who are interested in the subject are going to want to read the text and other sources of history. These turned-on students are going to want to read more, write more, and think more about how to solve the major problems we have faced throughout history. These are the kinds of students we want to be the decision makers of the future.

In these opening years of the twenty-first century, all of us are facing information overload. The amount of information in the world is doubling every year. The need now is not for more memorization of trivial facts from the past, but rather the development of skills in the analysis of this information to decipher what is important in making present and future decisions.

The thematic organization of each of the three units in this volume— *Enlightenment, The Nineteenth Century, and The Twentieth Century*—are designed to facilitate the development of historical skills in the analysis of this information critical for decision making. Each unit is organized into fourteen general historical themes for easy reference:

Theme	1	Historical Time Line
Theme	2	Separating Fact from Myth and Propaganda
Theme	3	Location and Movement
Theme	4	Politics and Leadership
Theme	5	Social and Economic Life
Theme	6	Religious Thought
Theme	7	Conquest and Warfare
Theme	8	Tragedy and Disaster

Theme 9   Exploration and Discovery
Theme 10   Invention and Revolution
Theme 11   Art and Creative Thought
Theme 12   Successes and Failure of an Era
Theme 13   Major Historical Problems
Theme 14   Era Antecedents for the Future

Within each of the above themes are the *Thematic Lesson Pacs* (TLPs). Each TLP has a short reading and a variety of creative multiple ways to study each theme. As a way of introduction, some of the major active learning strategies presented in each Thematic Lesson Pac (TLP) are as follows:

Quick Writes	Photo Analysis
Role Plays	Map Attacks
Viewpoints	Concept Webbing
Venn Diagrams	Quick Skits
T Charts	What If?
Time Lines	Spin Doctors
Pair Shares	Counter Spins
Diary Entries	Time Travelers
Poet Corners	Talk Show Hosts
Art Marts	Poster Power
Songs and Rap Fests	Quick Calcs
Front Page Newspapers	History Chains
Travel Brochures	Pros and Cons
Dioramas and Models	Research Projects
"You Were There" Interviews	Futurists
Slogans and Graffiti	Action Research
Bumper Stickers	Opinion Polls

For more innovative ideas on teaching and learning about world history, be sure to see volume 1 of *Breaking Away from the Textbook: Creative Ways to Teach World History,* which covers prehistory through the Renaissance. The appendices for both volumes provide a traditional chronological table of contents, map resources, recommended background music, and interesting CD-ROMs and Web sites for world history teachers and students.

It is the sincere desire of this author to have students excited about world history; from recent brain research, we know that students learn better when they are excited and interested in their studies. This series is far from complete when considering all of the possible topics to cover in world history. It is the wish of the author, however, that teachers use this volume as a starting point for their own creativity. Apply the teaching ideas from this volume to other topics in history. History does not have to be an endless list of dead men entombed between the covers of a textbook. Use this volume as a starting point to turn students on to world history. Such excitement can then have an amazing ripple effect. Teachers become more interested in teaching. Schools become more exciting places to be. More learning takes place, and suddenly the world is becoming a better place. It can be done.

—Ron H. Pahl

California State University, Fullerton

The Scientific Revolution and the Enlightenment (1600 to 1800)

UNIT 5: TABLE OF CONTENTS

INTRODUCTION

The Scientific Revolution and the Enlightenment

"Sapere aude!" wrote Immanuel Kant at the height of the Enlightenment in 1781—"Dare to know! Have the courage to use your own intelligence." Human ignorance is not caused by the lack of intelligence but from the "lack of determination and courage to use that intelligence without another's guidance."

The Enlightenment followed on the heels of the Renaissance. The Renaissance opened the door to reason for the first time in one thousand years. The Reformation reacted against this and restated the medieval belief in faith, but in so doing also aided the Enlightenment by weakening the Catholic Church in Rome. The Renaissance opened the door to reason, but had neither the courage nor the power to oppose the medieval concept of faith instead of reason. The leaders of the Enlightenment had that courage and power—Descartes in mathematics, Mozart in music, Rembrandt in painting, and Locke and Rousseau in politics. Revolution was in the air. The powerful old monarchies were rapidly crumbling. The English Revolutions of 1641 and 1688, the American Revolution of 1776, and the French Revolution of 1789 all brought the Enlightenment to a climax. The bloodbath of the French Revolution at the end of the eighteenth century, however, also caused people to question whether the Enlightenment had gone too far. Was too much trust placed in reason during the Enlightenment? Regardless of the answer, the Enlightenment produced a profound effect on the world. The government of the United States, elected governments across the world, capitalism, the idea of fundamental human rights, and even Marxism are the direct results of the Enlightenment. "Sapere aude!" wrote Kant, and the world still follows this motto of the Enlightenment: "Dare to know!"

THEMATIC LESSON PACS FOR THE SCIENTIFIC REVOLUTION AND THE ENLIGHTENMENT

5.1.0 HISTORICAL TIME LINE

5.1.1 A History Time Line of the Enlightenment

- Name Plates: Photocopy six sets of the fourteen names and items below. Cut each name or item into a strip of paper. Place the strips of paper carefully into separate envelopes for each team and label the envelopes "5.1.1 The Enlightenment History Time Line" for later use in class.
- Team Power: Break the class into six teams.
- The Envelope: Each team should be given an envelope containing the following random fourteen names from the Enlightenment:
  1. Wolfgang Amadeus Mozart born—1756
  2. The Bastille was stormed—1789
  3. Adam Smith wrote *Wealth of Nations*—1776

4. Descartes wrote *Discourse on Method*—1637
5. Thirty Years War—1618–1648
6. James Cook discovered Tahiti—1789
7. American Revolution—1776
8. Napoleon's coup d'etat in France—1799
9. Rousseau wrote *Social Contract*—1761
10. Blumbach invented concept of race—1776
11. Hans Lippershey invented the telescope—1608
12. William Shakespeare wrote *Macbeth*—1603
13. Cromwell's Puritans control England—1649
14. African slaves taken to Caribbean—1600

- Team Time Line: The first job of each team is to correctly order the fourteen names and artifacts according to time, with the oldest at the top and the most recent at the bottom. Each student should separately write the correct time line for the Enlightenment names and artifacts on a personal sheet of paper for later reference.
- Team Look Up: Once every member of the team has the Enlightenment time line on his or her own sheet of paper, each of the fourteen Enlightenment names should be divided between members of the team to find out the meaning of each name from their textbooks. Once found, the meanings of each Enlightenment name can be shared with the members of the team to write on their own time lines.
- Poster Power: On a large piece of paper, each team should construct its own time line for the Enlightenment using the fourteen names, with descriptions and illustrations to demonstrate the meaning of each name. When finished, these can be presented to the class and displayed on the classroom wall.
- Music Mart: Each team should pick what they think is the most important name or event in the time line and then compose and present a short song or rap about the name or event. When finished, this can be presented to the class for its approval.
- Journal Entry: Have each team member write a short journal entry speculating about what they now know about the development of humans during the Enlightenment (from the time line they developed) and possibly the most important things to happen during this era. When finished, students can first share their thoughts with their team and then with the class as a whole for general discussion about what they think are the most important things that happened during the era.

5.2.0   SEPARATING FACT FROM MYTH AND PROPAGANDA

5.2.1   Witchcraft during the Enlightenment

The Enlightenment is known for its commitment to reason and the beginnings of scientific exploration. The dark side of the Enlightenment, however, is that almost everyone during the Enlightenment continued to believe in witches and was willing to see witches killed. Between 1560 and 1600, some eight thousand elderly women were burned as witches in Scotland—a country of less than one million people. During the same period in England, under the rule of Elizabeth I, eighty-one women were executed for witchcraft. Within the two-year period of England's Long Parliament (1645–1647), two hundred witches were burned at the stake. Sociologically, the era of the Enlightenment in Europe was very tense, with Catholics and Protestants constantly battling each other—often in the same town. In almost all cases, the "witches" were elderly women who lived alone on the "other" side of town, with no one to support them and no one to get angry if they were killed. Someone would cry "witch"—there is no defense for an accusation of "witchcraft"—followed by more accusations of witchcraft until the town or community was exhausted from accusations and burnings. The "witch burnings" would then quickly die out. Why is it that even during the most enlightened periods of reason and education in history, the most primitive of human emotions and superstitions continue to exist (Durant and Durant 1961, 162–163)?

- Quick Witch: Describe in a short paragraph what you would do if someone accused you of witchcraft.
- Time Traveler: Imagine that you have traveled back in time to a witch burning in Elizabethan England. Describe the horror of what you see.
- Historical Analysis: Why do you think elderly women and not elderly men or young men were accused of witchcraft during the seventeenth century?
- ADV Civil Liberties: Using today's laws in the United States, what rights are guaranteed to a person falsely accused of a crime?
- ADV T Chart: Using a T chart, compare the rights of an elderly lady accused of witchcraft during the seventeenth century with the rights of a person standing trial for a crime today.

- ADV Historical Research: Trace the rise and fall of other forms of public hysteria and fears—similar to accusations of witchcraft—in recent history; for example, the anti-Communist hysteria of the 1950s in the United States.
- ADV The Futurist: Look through the news today for current media events that play on public hysteria and look very much like the "witch burning" patterns of the seventeenth century. Be sure to report your findings to the class.

5.2.2   John Locke and the Natural Human

As all other members of the Enlightenment, Locke saw that the Indians in America were in a perfect society of nature because they did not have to work and food was easy for them to obtain. As all people of reason believed, according to Locke, the Indians were closer to animals than people of reason because they did not have to work for their food. In that they were closer to animals, therefore, than reasonable people, wrote Locke, if they attacked reasonable people (Europeans), they could be attacked and killed in return.

John Locke's "reasonable" defense of the treating of non-Europeans as animals provided the intellectual support for the "scientific" racism of the nineteenth and twentieth centuries. It also provided the intellectual rationale for colonialism of the non-European nations by Europe. Locke's "reasonable" racism and colonialism, however, was not based entirely on intellect. Locke worked for Lord Shaftesbury, who was a part owner of slave ships and an active government official in colonization efforts in America. Locke himself was a direct investor in the Royal Africa Company and the Bahama Adventurers colonial merchant and slave trading companies founded by Shaftesbury in 1697 (Hulme and Jordanova 1990, 28–34).

- Quick Write: Give an example of a time when someone you know was treated unfairly. Why do you think they were treated unfairly? What do you think should have happened?
- Analysis: From the above reading, what did John Locke gain by reasoning that non-Europeans could be treated like animals?
- Time Traveler: Traveling back in time to the Enlightenment as a Native American Indian, how would you have reacted to John Locke's

reasoning about you? What would you have done in reaction to this line of "Enlightenment" reasoning?

- Poster Power: As a Native American Indian, create a poster that illustrates your impression of John Locke.
- ADV Research: Racism was a major problem during the nineteenth and twentieth centuries. What influence do you think John Locke's views had on the "racism" that developed in the United States and Europe during the nineteenth and twentieth centuries? Report your findings to the class.

5.2.3 Frankenstein and the Enlightenment

Although Mary Shelly's *Frankenstein* was written after the Enlightenment (during the nineteenth century), it is a novel of the Enlightenment. Frankenstein was a brilliant doctor who—in good Enlightenment fashion—tried to create a perfect human being out of the best human parts he could find; instead, he produced the ultimate monster. Members of the Enlightenment in Europe during the eighteenth century tried to reasonably create the best possible world for all (European) humans. Dr. Frankenstein was very carefully trying to do this very same thing. He wanted to create the perfect human being—out of body parts. Where could his brilliant thinking possibly have gone wrong?

- Quick Write: Describe what you remember of the story of *Frankenstein* in a short paragraph.
- Bumper Sticker: Create a bumper sticker warning people of the work of Dr. Frankenstein.
- Poster Power: Create a scary poster of Frankenstein illustrating its meaning in terms of the Enlightenment.
- Time Traveler: Go back in time and express your emotions as Frankenstein—knowing that you were created out of human parts. Use song or poetry to express the strength of your emotions if you wish.
- ADV Futurist: Research the central Enlightenment issue presented in *Frankenstein* and compare it to the growing issue of cloning of human beings during the twenty-first century.
- ADV Film Critic: See the film *Blade Runner* and compare it to any version of *Frankenstein*. Compare how both films treat the issue of artificial human beings.

5.3.0 LOCATION AND MOVEMENT

5.3.1 The Problem of Longitude

As late as 1707, sailors—including admirals—did not know how to measure longitude. Late in that year, Admiral Shovell's English fleet was returning to England after battling the French. Close to the English coast and in dense fog, the admiral's fleet had no idea where they were. A sailor—who had begun to calculate location on his own—approached the admiral and warned him that he thought the fleet was dangerously close to the rocks along the Isles of Scilley. The admiral hanged the sailor on the spot for mutiny. True to the sailor's prediction, within a few hours, the fleet ran aground on the Isles of Scilley and more than two thousand men were lost at sea. In 1714, in response to this tragedy, the English Parliament offered a prize of $12 million to anyone who could create an accurate timepiece to measure longitude accurately. Telling accurate time with clocks was the end result of Admiral Shovell's folly in 1707. William Harrison achieved this feat fifty years later with the invention of his portable chronometer (clock).

- Quick Write: In a short paragraph, imagine life without a clock; what would it be like?
- T Chart: Make a list on one side of the T chart of all the things that require precise time. On the other side of the T chart, list what would happen without a precise method of keeping time.
- Short Skit: With a group of four students, create a short skit illustrating the incident between Admiral Shovell and the sailor.
- A Letter Home: As a sailor who witnessed the incident between Admiral Shovell and the sailor—and lived to tell about it—describe the incident as you saw it and your feelings about it.
- News Flash: As the ace reporter of the *Enlightenment Times* newspaper, you were the first on the scene when Admiral Shovell's fleet crashed into the Isles of Scilley in 1707. Describe what you saw.
- ADV Tick Tock: Put together a paper clock and describe how it works to your class. Note: Inexpensive paper clock kits are available at most large toy stores.
- ADV Historical Research: Trace the history of keeping time (for example, sundials, water clocks, hourglasses, and atomic clocks). How have these different time-keeping tools changed history?

- ADV Timelessness: The famous physicist Stephen Hawking in *A Brief History of Time* (1988) says that the concept of "time" is created by humans and that "time" itself does not exist in the universe. What implications does Hawking's discovery have for human history?

5.4.0 POLITICS AND LEADERSHIP

5.4.1 *Que sais-je?*—What Do I Know?

Michel de Montaigne (1533–1592) loved his library and loved to write essays; many say he invented essays. He lit the lamp of reason for the Enlightenment in Europe. Above all, said Montaigne, we must keep an open mind about everything and not be trapped in dogmatic thinking. "The for and against are both possible . . . I suspend judgment; I examine . . . I fasten myself on that which I see and hold, and go not far from the shore" (Durant and Durant 1961).

Montaigne taught tolerance in an age of intolerance during the Thirty Years War. He continually tried to see all points of view. Where did he get such tolerance in such a brutal age? His mother was Spanish, born Jewish but baptized as a Protestant Christian; his father was a pious Catholic.

He was openly critical of reason, but was one of the first practitioners of reason. He was openly critical of Christianity, but remained a Christian. He saw no need to change governments, because he saw all governments as corrupt. He refused to fight in war—but was one of the first to promote compromise. Durant speaks of him: "Montaigne was the most civilized of Frenchmen in that savage age" (Durant and Durant 1961, 399–415).

Note from the Future: The list of Enlightenment thinkers influenced by Montaigne is impressive: Bacon, Descartes, Shakespeare, Voltaire, Locke, and Rousseau. Even today, he remains one of the most powerful voices in history for reason, tolerance, and moderation.

- Quick Fight: In a short paragraph, describe a recent fight you saw between two students. Why did they fight? Describe the views of both students who were fighting. How could the fight have been prevented?
- T Chart: With a partner, fill out one side of a T chart with reasons why your country should fight a war. On the other side of the T chart,

fill out counter reasons why your country should not fight a war. What conclusions can you draw from your T chart? In what way are these conclusions similar to those of Montaigne?

- Bumper Sticker: Create a bumper sticker supporting Montaigne's point of view during the Thirty Years War.
- Meet the Press: You are the host of the top TV show during the Enlightenment, and your guest today is Montaigne (the teacher in costume or a well-prepared student), to be interviewed by the top reporters of the day (students in the class). Due to the lack of time for this very important guest, reporters will be limited to only one question each. Questions can be concerning religion, the raging Thirty Years War, the importance of reason, or anything Montaigne wrote about in his famous essays.
- Poster Power: Create a poster illustrating Montaigne's enormous influence on the Enlightenment and supporters of moderation today.
- ADV Futurist: Montaigne would have been an excellent war protestor during any recent military conflict. Pick a recent or current war and organize a war protest based on Montaigne's thinking.

5.4.2   The English Coup d'etat (1649)

In 1641, the Protestant English Parliament wanted power but the Catholic King Charles I would not give it to them. The split divided England. The Catholic North and West sided with the king. The Protestant East and South supported the Protestant Parliament. Oliver Cromwell (1599–1658), a Puritan who planned to become a colonist in Massachusetts, instead created a Puritan army to fight for Parliament. With no military experience, Cromwell created the world's first tightly organized modern army composed of commoners—not nobles. Supported by returning Puritan troops from America, his army—"the Roundheads"—routed the royal forces and captured the king. But why stop with the king? In a coup d'etat, Cromwell's army also seized Parliament and dismissed all members who did not support Cromwell. The new "Rump Parliament of Cromwell" now declared itself "the supreme power in this nation" and promptly put the king on trial for treason against Parliament. When Cromwell and his Rump Parliament signed the king's death warrant, all of England—Protestant and Catholic—cried out against it. Eyewitnesses said all of England groaned in sadness when the king's head was chopped off.

Note from the Future: The execution of the king revolted all of England—except the Puritans; within eleven years, a king was back on the throne. It took a less violent revolution in 1688 to establish the English Parliament as supreme, but with a king at the head of England's government. The monarchy in England has not been questioned since (Durant and Durant 1961, 207–221).

- Quick Right: Who do you think has more power in the United States—the president, Congress, or the military? Write a short paragraph describing your opinion.
- Poster Power: Create a poster supporting the king, Parliament, or the Roundheads.
- Short Skit: With four students, create a skit that illustrates the problems between Cromwell's army, Parliament, and the king of England.
- The Queen's Commission: Queen Henrietta is tired of all the arguing between the king and Parliament. She has asked your class to assemble small study teams of four each to develop plans by which the king and Parliament could work out a compromise to prevent the upcoming English civil war. Have each group present its plan to the assembled class. As a class, develop an overall plan to present to the queen.
- Bumper Sticker: Create a bumper sticker that either supports the death penalty and Cromwell or supports the king and opposes the death penalty.
- ADV Futurist: Research how England's early parliamentary government—rather than absolute rule by the king and nobles—encouraged the early agricultural and industrial revolutions in England.
- ADV Future Problem: What threat exists in the United States of the military taking control of the government, as it has in so many other countries? What means does the United States have to protect itself from a takeover by the military?

5.4.3   The Baron of Montesquieu

Charles de Secondat, Baron de Montesquieu (1689–1755)—Montesquieu for short—was one of the earliest Enlightenment philosophers to call for an end to despotism. Freedom for the individual was his goal for government. To achieve freedom, he saw the need for a government to have a constitution to guarantee the safety and security of the individual. He also saw the need to divide the responsibilities of government (in order to secure individual freedom) between three separate and independent branches of government—the executive, the legislative, and the judicial. He also condemned all forms of cruel punishment and the torture of prisoners. Montesquieu's concept of individual freedom distinguished between a person's actions and a person's thoughts. A law may state that it is illegal to overthrow a government—an action. A government, says Montesquieu, may not, however, make laws that make it illegal *to think* about overthrowing a government (Gay 1966, 57–59).

- Quick Right: Write a short paragraph describing the major means by which the United States government guarantees the freedom of the individual.
- Bumper Sticker: Create a bumper sticker supporting one or more of the rights called for by Montesquieu.
- Poster Power: Create a poster illustrating the major rights called for by Montesquieu.
- T-Chart: Compare the rights called for by Montesquieu and the basic organization of the United States government.
- One Name Answer: Upon whom did Madison, Hamilton, and Jay base the basic organization of the United States government after the American Revolution? (Hint: He was a French baron.)
- ADV Historical Research: Which principles of government described by Montesquieu did the Founding Fathers of the United States Constitution *not* adopt? Why not? Of the principles of government adopted by the Founding Fathers, which were *not* described by Montesquieu? Describe why.

5.4.4   July 14, 1789

Aristocratic France did not realize rebellion was in the air. The nobles argued about Montesquieu, Voltaire, and Locke in their grand palaces—but did not do anything to help the common people. They applauded the American Revolution (1776–1781) for implementing the ideals of the Enlightenment and used their military armies and fleets to ensure the American victory against the English.

Everybody in the French nobility cheered the success of the American Revolution—but paid no attention to governmental reform and the needs of the common people of France. The French government had huge debts to pay for aiding the American Revolution against England. Several wet years had ruined crops and the wine harvests across the country. The initial conditions for revolution were in place. Still, the French nobility ignored the common people. The date was July 14, 1789; a Parisian crowd rose up and captured the Bastille, the main prison in Paris. It was the beginning of the French Revolution. The commoners in France were beginning their move to take control of their own country.

During the last ten years of the eighteenth century, the French citizenry revolted, killed a king, established a republic, and had a coup d'etat led by Napoleon Bonaparte in 1799. Somehow, through it all, the ideals of the Enlightenment remained together—roughed up perhaps, but together (Gay 1966, 164–168).

- Quick Right: At what point do you think a group of people has the right to rebel against their government?
- Bumper Sticker: Design and create a carriage bumper sticker either for or against the French Revolution.
- Poster Power: Create a large poster calling for the French peasants to rise up and support the French Revolution.
- Cheer Leaders: Imagine that you are a fanatical patriot of the French Revolution. Create a rousing cheer to convince other French men and women—your classmates—to join the revolution.
- ADV Historical Analysis: Using the resources in your library, make a list of all the contributing factors you can find that led to the French Revolution.
- ADV What If?: In teams of four students, devise a plan to prevent the French Revolution and present it to the assembled people of France (your class).
- ADV Futurist: As a class, compare current conditions in the United States to see if there is any similarity to the initial conditions leading up to the French Revolution. Based on your analysis, what are the chances of a major revolution taking place in the United States in the near future?

5.4.5   Human Rights—Eternal or Evolving?

During the American and French Revolutions, such leading revolutionaries as Thomas Paine saw that human rights were eternal and unchanging.

The revolutionaries believed that these unchanging rights (such as freedom of speech, freedom of the press, and freedom of assembly) were goals to be fought for until they were achieved. These rights, as stated in the *Declaration of the Rights of Man* (1789) became the cause for which the leaders of the American and French Revolutions fought their battles. Edmond Burke, in England, strongly disagreed with the revolutionaries who were ready to die for their eternal human rights. Human rights, said Burke, were not fixed eternal goals for a revolution. Human rights, said Burke, were rather very human things that continually change and evolve. To Burke, killing others to achieve human rights was a contradiction. Burke believed that human rights are achieved slowly and piece by piece through new laws and by slowly changing the way people think. The Enlightenment, therefore, posed a fundamental question to humanity: Do we achieve human rights through a revolution (as desired by Thomas Paine) or do we work slowly and change these human rights step-by-step (as desired by Edmond Burke)?

- Quick Right: What do you think is the most important right we have as humans? Can we exercise this right anywhere in the world? Why not?
- Poster Power: Create a poster illustrating your most important right.
- T Chart: Compare the methods of how human rights should be obtained—by violent revolution (Paine) or by slow change (Burke).
- Speech Writers: Thomas Paine and Edmond Burke have to give speeches in the near future and have asked you to write their speeches for them. In teams of two, write a speech for either Paine or Burke and present it to the class, focusing on how each plans to implement human rights.
- ADV Historical Comparison: Compare Paine's and Burke's methods of implementing human rights across history. Which method do you think has been the most effective in the long run? Explain your reasons why.

5.4.6   How Not to Run a Revolution

Revolutions are hard to control and the French Revolution was no exception. The Revolution (1789–1794) took place in two phases, which were very different from each other. The first was a moderate phase headed by Comte de Mirabeau. Mirabeau tried to model his form of government on that developed by the English, with a national assembly of all people and a moderate king at the top of the government. Under Mirabeau (and with the help of Thomas Jefferson), an assembly of all French people wrote the *Declaration of the Rights of Man,* which declared that all people have the basic freedoms of expression, representation, and due process of law.

But Mirabeau's moderate revolution was neither supported by the king or nobles, who thought it went too far, nor by the radicals under Maximilien Robespierre, who thought it did not go far enough. Threatened with outside invasions from Austria, Spain, and England and by unrest across France, Robespierre and the radical "Committee of Public Safety" were given dictatorial power to bring France under control. Under Robespierre's one-year "Reign of Terror," approximately 30,000 people went to the guillotine on charges that they were counterrevolutionaries. The king and queen were killed, as were any nobles who were caught, and any commoners who were under suspicion of being traitors. The terror of the radicals worked. The violence subsided and the last to lose his head to the guillotine in 1794 was Robespierre himself. The Revolution was over with a new republican government now ruling France.

- Quick Write: If you were the leader of a revolution, describe how you would conduct your revolution in a short paragraph.
- Poster Power: Create a poster either supporting Mirabeau or Robespierre in the French Revolution.
- Model It: Create a miniature working model of the guillotine and demonstrate how it works—on nonliving things.
- Venn Diagram: Compare the differences and similarities in the French Revolution under the rules of Mirabeau with those of Robespierre.
- Role Play #1: Divide the class into quads (groups of four) of moderates and groups of radicals during the French Revolution. Have each group create a plan for taking control of the Revolution and keeping control. Each group can then report to the class on their plan and compare plans with those of the other groups.
- Role Play #2:
  Step One: Pick one of the following roles during the French Revolution.
  1. Nobility: Count LeMan (male), Countess LeMan (female)
  2. Church Person: Father Paras (m), Sister Paras (f)

3. Middle Class: Storekeeper Mavon (m), daughter Mavonna (f)
4. Military: Sergeant Labonn (m), Nurse Labonn (f)
5. Peasant: Grizelda (f), Grizmald (m)

Step Two: Pick one of the sides of the Revolution.

1. Strongly anti-revolutionary, supporting the nobility
2. Moderately revolutionary, supporting Mirabeau and king
3. Radically revolutionary, supporting Robespierre

Step Three: Decide how you are going to support your side during the Revolution without losing your head in the guillotine.

- ADV Historical Comparison: Compare the French Revolution with the English Revolution under Cromwell (1649) and the American Revolution (1776).
- ADV Futurist: Devise a plan for leading and controlling a future revolution in the United States. Share your plans with the class.

5.5.0   SOCIAL AND ECONOMIC LIFE

5.5.1   Adam Smith: How Does a Nation Become Rich?

During most of the Enlightenment, the governments of Europe believed that the nation holding the most resources was the richest state. Each government tried to control as many raw materials, cheap skilled workers, and factories as they could at the expense of the other countries. This economic system was called *mercantilism*. These mercantilist governments believed that there was a set amount of money and wealth in the world. Divide it up and the country with the most wins. The growing race for colonies across the world was based on this mercantile idea.

In 1776, Adam Smith wrote *Wealth of Nations* and broke away from the idea of strict governmental control of the economy. He called his economic system "the invisible hand of self-interest" or "laissez-faire." The goal of Smith's *Wealth of Nations* was to enrich the people and the government at the same time by opening up the whole economic system. Wealth, to Smith, was not a fixed amount of resources to be kept locked up in a vault but an open system of using existing resources to their fullest to make and sell products to as many people as possible with as little governmental control as possible. Workers, according to Smith, should be paid high wages, not low wages, to make them more productive and give them more money to buy products in the economy. The person, company, or country with the most items sold is the wealthiest, according to Adam Smith (Gay 1966, 104–105).

Note from the Future: Europe's rush to grab colonies across the world during the nineteenth century was based on the out-of-date idea of mercantilism. The economic growth of the United States during the twentieth century was based on Adam Smith's laissez-faire economics or capitalism.

- Quick Rich: Think for a moment and then present an idea how you can make a lot of money legally. When finished, describe how you will know when you are rich.
- Bumper Sticker: Make an Enlightenment bumper sticker supporting either mercantilism or Adam Smith's laissez-faire economic system.
- Front Page: As the editors of the *Enlightenment Times* newspaper, in teams of four students each, write and lay out a front-page special edition for 1776 describing the radical new ideas of Adam Smith and how they conflict with mercantilism. Be sure to include interviews, illustrations, and big two-inch headlines in your edition.
- ADV Historical Comparison: Compare the historical impact mercantile and laissez-faire economics have had on the world.
- ADV Futurist #1: Capitalists today favor paying their workers low wages to increase their personal profits. Contrast this view with the original views of Adam Smith in 1776.
- ADV Futurist #2: Devise an economic model that is neither mercantile nor laissez-faire.

5.5.2 Blumbach's *Categories of Race* (1776)

Jefferson's *Declaration of Independence* was written in 1776. Adam Smith's *Wealth of Nations* was written in 1776. Blumbach's categories of "races" were also written in 1776. All three events had a major influence on the world of the nineteenth and twentieth centuries. Blumbach's work, however, had a strongly negative effect on the world. Prior to Blumbach, all humans were considered to belong to the same race—the human race. Shakespeare, Milton, Spencer, and other English writers before Blumbach always referred to a single human race. Blumbach studied human skulls and from his study concluded that a female skull from the Caucus Mountains in Russia was "the most beautiful." Based on this study of skull beauty, Blumbach created a "Caucasian Race" of European humans, which he thought superior to "the other human races": the "Asian Race," the "American Indian Race," and the "African Race."

Note from the Future: Blumbach made no other comments concerning his "different human races" other than skull beauty. Other nineteenth century "scientists," however, used Blumbach's "racial" categories to create a whole justification for slavery and discrimination against non-Europeans during the nineteenth and twentieth centuries (Pahl 1997, 12–17).

- Quick Write: In your own words, describe why you think some people discriminate against other people.
- Cartoon It: Make a cartoon of Blumbach's original classification of different "races" by skull beauty in 1776.
- Concept Web: As a class activity, make a concept web describing how many different ways human beings can be compared (for example, eye color, height, fingernail length).
- What If?: Have students classify themselves according to different things, such as favorite pizza toppings, favorite sport teams, and favorite TV shows. The teacher should then assign (false) grades (A–F) to students based on their favorite pizza topping, sports team, and TV show.
- Share Pair: Students in a share pair (following the above What If) can then discuss the implications of such a grading system and the implications of classifying different humans into any categories. These discussions can then be shared with the class.
- Cultural Comparison: In groups of four, compare different cultures and ethnic groups by foods, clothes, languages, and skin color. Discuss the fairness of classifying any person on the basis of these items and then discriminating against that person based on such a classification.
- ADV Historical Analysis: Using your library and the Internet, research attempts by "scientists" to classify humans by different physical traits in the past and report to the class on your findings.
- ADV TV Action Research: Track the use of the word "race" by TV announcers over several weeks and count how many times the word

is used in a positive context and how many times in a negative context. What are your findings and the implications of your findings? (Past studies have shown a very high negative context for almost all uses of the word on TV.)
- ADV Action Planning: As a class, make an action plan on how to use or not use the word "race" in the future.

5.5.3 Islamic Literacy

Most Europeans during the Enlightenment were still uneducated. The ideas of the Enlightenment were strictly for the literate nobility in Europe. Even though the reading of the Bible by individuals was a major idea to come out of the Reformation, personal reading of the Qur'an by Muslims had been established at the beginning of Islam, almost one thousand years earlier. By 1600, the result was a very large Muslim literate population spread across the world—far larger than Europe's literate population. This literate Muslim population did not read just the Qur'an. In 1648, Hajji Khalfah compiled a list of over 25,000 books in Arabic, Turkish, and Persian on such widely diverse topics as theology, law, science, medicine, biography, and history. The first universities of the world were Islamic universities during the Middle Ages, and continued to be prominent in such widely diverse Muslim countries as Morocco, Egypt, Turkey, and Iraq (Durant and Durant 1961, 518–526).

- Quick Write: In a short paragraph, briefly describe the advantages a literate person has over an illiterate person.
- Bumper Sticker: Create an Enlightenment bumper sticker to encourage peasants to learn how to read and write.
- Counter Spin: In a short paragraph, briefly describe the advantages an illiterate person has over a literate person.
- Letter Writing: As a time traveler to an Islamic university in Egypt during the Enlightenment, write a letter home describing how advanced Muslim education is at the time compared to that in Europe.
- T-Chart: On a T chart, compare the level of education in Europe and the Islamic world during the Enlightenment.
- Ad Campaign: In teams of four, create an ad campaign to encourage peasants around the world to read and write. Include a TV jingle, a thirty-second ad spot, and a poster to put up on the wall. Be careful, however—the nobles want to keep the peasants ignorant and uneducated and may give you some trouble.

- ADV Historical Comparison: Using your library and the Internet, re-search the reasons why literacy rates during the Enlightenment were higher in the Islamic world than in Christian Europe. Report your findings to your class.

5.6.0   RELIGIOUS THOUGHT

5.6.1   Predestination, Free Will, and Communion Wine

John Calvin (1509–1564) from Geneva, Switzerland, was a Protestant, as was Luther—but Calvin was much stricter. Where Luther believed that humans had the "free will" to decide whether they had faith in God, Calvin said that only God could determine who would be saved and who would not be saved. There was no human "free will." God "predestined" everything that happens on Earth. Local Calvinist churches elected their own leaders and had the authority to make sure that their congregations strictly followed the word of the Bible. Any who sinned were strictly punished—even by being burnt at the stake. In a revival of the icono-clasts of the Middle Ages, Calvinists proceeded to destroy any church images they could find—statues, stained-glass windows, even the image of the cross. In opposition to both the Catholics and Lutherans, the Calvinists did not believe the wine of communion turned into blood. The Lutherans tolerated much of the Calvinist theology, but disagreed bitterly about the nature of the communion wine. On this small point of theology, the Lutherans and Calvinists broke from each other. The split made an absolute mess of the Thirty Years War because the Protestants were fighting as much among themselves as they were against the Catholics (Durant and Durant 1961, 551–556).

- Quick Write: What is your opinion? Do you think that humans have the right to choose their God? Or does a divine being choose your fate, whether or not you believe in God? Explain your answer.
- Bumper Sticker: Create a bumper sticker for either Lutheran or Calvinist troops to carry into battle during the Thirty Years War.
- Venn Diagram: Create a Venn diagram that illustrates the similarities and differences between Lutheran and Calvinist Protestants.
- Poster Power: Create a poster that either supports John Calvin or Martin Luther. Make sure it illustrates one or more of the key beliefs of one of these major leaders of the Reformation.

- ADV Historical Research: Trace the influence of the Calvinist churches in the settling of the American colonies.

5.6.2   The Puritans

The Calvinists in England began to be called "Puritans" (a term of abuse) around 1564 by the more moderate Protestants in the Anglican Church of England. The Puritans demanded strict conformity to their interpretation of the Bible and harsh physical punishment to all sinners who disobeyed their rules. The Puritans began to hold separate church services and became very popular. By 1593, Queen Elizabeth I saw their growing power as much a threat to her rule as that of the Catholics. In that year, she had Parliament pass a law requiring that no one could question the queen's religious authority as head of the church. Those who attended any religious services other than the Church of England should be punished, forced to leave the country, and be banned from returning on penalty of death. The Puritans began to get the message and the more radical ones left the country to eventually settle at a lonely outpost called Plymouth Rock, in what would become Massachusetts. Later, however, after Elizabeth's death, the Puritans grabbed control of Parliament, killed King Charles I, and ruled England as a republic with strict Puritan rules under Thomas Cromwell (Durant and Durant 1961, 23–27).

- Quick Write: If you opposed certain rules of your government, how would you show your opposition to these rules without being thrown in jail?
- Ad Campaign: In teams of four, develop an ad campaign for either the Puritans or the Church of England under Queen Elizabeth I. Be sure to include a poster, a TV jingle, and thirty-second spot promoting your sponsor.
- Role Play: Stage a short skit of Queen Elizabeth meeting the leaders of the Puritans. What would they say to each other? What would be the outcomes of such a meeting?
- If You Were There: If you were the queen of England, how would you handle the Puritans who were a constant thorn in your side?
- ADV Venn Diagram: Compare the differences and similarities between the Puritans and the Church of England under Queen Elizabeth I.

- ADV T Chart: Compare the basic rights of religious freedom we have today with the lack of religious rights under both the Church of England and the Puritans.
- ADV The Futurist: Research current news media for signs of modern threats to religious freedoms at home and across the world.

5.6.3   Tolerant Islam

The European Enlightenment had little or no effect on the Muslim world. Islam was a very egalitarian religion from its beginnings in 622; everyone was taught how to read the Qur'an. The feudal hierarchy of Europe, with its tight division between nobles and peasants, did not exist in the Muslim world. Furthermore, a church hierarchy did not dominate Islam for a thousand years, as one did in Christianity. The result was that the Muslim world was a religion still strong in its roots with no calls for a Reformation or an Enlightenment. Where religious intolerance dominated the Enlightenment in Europe between Catholic, Lutheran, and Calvinist beliefs, religious tolerance was widely practiced across the Islamic world. Although taxed more heavily as non-Muslims, Protestants, Catholics, Coptics (in Egypt), Greek Orthodox, and Jews were allowed to practice their religions without interference. Persecuted Jews fleeing from Spain and Europe often fled to Muslim-ruled Turkey to safely practice their religion. Some Protestants in eastern European countries such as Hungary openly supported the Muslim Turkish rule, while the Catholic ruler of the Holy Roman Empire in Austria did not (Durant and Durant 1961, 518–526).

- Quick Write: In your own words, describe why you think people of different religions are intolerant of each other.
- T Chart: Compare Christianity and Islam in terms of religious change and tolerance to other religions.
- Poster Power: Create a poster illustrating the intolerance of the Christian churches and the tolerance of other religious communities by the Muslims during the Enlightenment.
- Newspaper Special Edition: In teams of four, create a front-page special edition reporting on the Jews being expelled by the Christians in Spain and being accepted by the Muslim rulers of the Ottoman Empire in Turkey. Be sure to include interviews with newly arrived Jewish refugees in the Ottoman Empire.

- ADV Futurist #1: Research the Jews fleeing the Nazi holocaust during the twentieth century and being accepted again by the Muslim Turks.
- ADV Futurist #2: Research your library and the Internet to find out the sources of the widespread religious intolerance by Jews, Christians, and Muslims during the twentieth century. When finished, report your findings to the class.

5.7.0 CONQUEST AND WARFARE

5.7.1 Thirty Years War (1618–1648)

Before 1618, the Lutherans, Calvinists, and the Catholics were in the middle of a large-scale cold war of pamphlets full of slanderous accusations—most of them false—against each other.

In 1618, this all changed. In Prague, a Protestant mob grabbed the Catholic governors of the state and threw them out the window of the castle into a dung pile below. The Catholic governors, unhurt but rather dirty and insulted, demanded that the Protestant mob be immediately punished. Catholic and Protestant rulers across Europe quickly began to take sides in the dispute, form alliances, and build their armies. Most of the leaders of the Protestant mob in Prague were beheaded by the Catholics and their heads displayed above the main bridge in Prague. All of Europe immediately went to war. Ironically, in the thirty years of brutal warfare between the Lutherans, Calvinists, and Catholics, Prague was the only major town that was not destroyed in the war. It should be recalled that Prague was where the war actually started when some Protestants threw the Catholic governors in the dung pile. Note: The excuses for going to war are often very strange.

After thirty years of warfare, all the battle-weary forces reluctantly sat down; after a seemingly endless debate, they signed the Peace of Westphalia (1648). The treaty basically divided up Europe into the Protestant and Catholic states we know today. Most of northern Europe remained Protestant; most of southern Europe remained Catholic. What was not mentioned in the peace treaty was Christianity. Everybody was tired of the endless religious polemics and the brutality of warfare for thirty years done in the name of Christianity. Also in the name of Christianity, thousands of innocent women were burned as witches during the war. Europe, after the Thirty Years War, wanted to try something different—reason rather than religion. The door of history was open for the Enlightenment (Durant and Durant 1961, 556–572).

- Quick Write: Make a list of all the reasons you can think of why people and countries go to war with each other.
- Share Pair: With a partner, share your lists of reasons why people go to war. From these lists, make a list of reasons that you both think are good and just reasons for anybody to go to war.
- War Council: In groups of four, with your lists of good and just reasons for war, decide how long a war should last when neither side can be victorious. How many resources will be needed to just maintain basic survival in such a war? How many years can you last? How many people have to be killed? How many towns and homes destroyed?
- Cartoonist: Draw a cartoon of the incident that caused the Thirty Years War—the governors being thrown in the dung pile.
- Role Play: Role-play the Protestant and Catholic leaders of Europe in 1618. Bring them (students) to the peace table and decide (as a class) how to prevent the Thirty Years War—one of the bloodiest and most destructive in history.
- ADV Map Attack: From resources in your library, map out the Thirty Years War: Prague, where it began; the Catholic and Protestant states of Europe; and Westphalia, where it ended.
- ADV Historical Analysis: Read in your library about the history of warfare and analyze why major wars are often fought over such little things.

5.8.0 TRAGEDY AND DISASTER

5.8.1 The Tragedy of Sugar Cane (1600)

The word "sugar" comes from the Arabic "sukkar" and was introduced to the Europeans from the Middle East after the Crusades. The introduction of sugar to Europe caused a sensation—everybody wanted it. The Europeans, however, did not have a hot tropical location to grow it properly. Columbus introduced sugar cane into the Americas in 1493, and it grew rapidly in the Caribbean Islands. The troops of Cortez were growing sugarcane successfully in Mexico by 1520 and it spread quickly to Puerto Rico, Venezuela, and Brazil. The aim was to export it for huge profits back to Europe. The major problem was that the laborers in the sugar cane fields—the Native Americans—were dying too fast from the European diseases. The "humanitarian" Spanish priest De Las Casas suggested bringing African laborers to the Americas to work the sugarcane, instead of the Native Americans. By 1600, more than one million African slaves were imported to the Americas to work on the sugar plantations in Brazil, the Caribbean, and Mexico (Manley 1992, 70).

- Quick Slave: Close your eyes for a moment and imagine being locked in irons on your hands and feet and being sold as a slave. Write a short paragraph describing how it feels to be a slave.
- Role Play: Sugar cane grows in twelve- to fifteen-foot-tall reeds that are often two inches wide. In groups of four, role-play African slaves toiling all day under the hot tropical sun cutting sugarcane with a sharp machete. Describe in your role-play how slaves can survive such hard work when escape is almost impossible on a small tropical island in the Caribbean.
- Front-Page Edition: In teams of four, create a special front-page edition of the *Enlightenment Times* newspaper describing the slave trade to the Americas to grow sugar for Europe. Include big headlines, drawings, and interviews with slave traders and slaves working in the fields (students in your class).
- You Were There: As the host of this popular TV program, have the members of your audience (students) ask your panel members about the slave trade. Your panel members (students in full costume) are as follows:
  1. Bertrum Gritch—the peg-legged master of the slave ship *Brisbane*
  2. Lolly Deeter—owner of London's most famous tea and pastry shop, and buyer of large quantities of sugar
  3. Ogun Warree—a recently enslaved African from Nigeria who toils in the sugar fields
  4. Nellie Smith—the wife of the owner of a plantation that grows sugar on the island of St. Croix in the Caribbean
  5. Nat—the escaped slave who is hiding in the mountains and trying to get other slaves to join him in rebelling against the European plantation owners
- ADV Historical Research: Using your library, research how individuals develop the negative attitudes and beliefs strong enough to enslave another human being. Report your findings to the class.

5.9.0   EXPLORATION AND DISCOVERY

5.9.1   Galileo: The Starry Messenger (1609)

Galileo (1564–1642) radically changed our human understanding of the universe. The Polish astronomer Copernicus had wisely waited until after his own death in 1543 to allow a report to be published that stated the sun—not the Earth—was the center of the solar system. The Church declared Copernicus a heretic and burned his books. Galileo believed that if he proved that Copernicus was correct by direct observation through his telescope, everyone would accept it as the truth— *big* mistake. He used his telescope to see four moons of Jupiter, craters on the moon, and the phases of Venus' orbit around the sun, and in 1609 published his book, *The Starry Messenger,* which supported Copernicus' theory. The book was an immediate sensation across Europe, except in the Vatican. The pope formally banned it and Galileo was required to remain silent on the topic for twenty-three years. Finally, in 1632, when he was seventy years old, he published *Dialogue on the Great World Systems,* in which he staged a debate between himself— supporting the church—and two supporters of Copernicus. The Church had enough of Mr. Galileo. He was called before the Inquisition. His orders were as follows: "His Holiness charges the Inquisitor in Florence to inform Galileo, in the name of the Holy Office, that he is to appear as soon as possible in the course of the month of October at Rome before the Commissary-General of the Holy Office (The Inquisition)." Obviously shaking in fear of being tortured on the rack, Galileo— seventy years old—sat in front of the black-robed judges of the dreaded Inquisition in Rome. Under such a threat, the old man recanted and denied his scientific discoveries in the heavens. From Codex 1181 in the Vatican Secret Archives, we have the exact words of his confession:

> I, Galileo, son of the late Vincenzio Galilei of Florence, my age being seventy years, . . . do swear that I have always believed, do now believe, and with God's aid shall believe hereafter all that which is taught and preached by the Holy Catholic and Apostolic Church. . . . I am by this Holy Office judged vehemently suspect of heresy; that is, of having held and believed that the Sun is the center of the world and immovable, and that the Earth is not its center and moves. Therefore . . . I do abjure, damn, and detest the said errors and heresies . . . and I do swear for the future that I shall never again speak or assert, orally or in writing, such things as might bring me under similar suspicion. (Bronowski 1973)

Galileo's trial by the Inquisition definitely slowed down, but did not stop, the coming Enlightenment. His contemporary, and a father of the Enlightenment, René Descartes, fled from France to Sweden to continue his work there.

Note from the Future: The Church kept its ban on the works of Galileo for 200 years (Bronowski 1973, 196–218; Durant and Durant 1961, 600–612).

- Quick Write: Imagine you are told you cannot speak about something you know is true. How would you feel? What would you do about this situation? Write a short paragraph about the situation.
- Quick Skit: With four partners, create a short skit illustrating Galileo's conflict with the Inquisition.
- Diary Entry: As Galileo, write a series of diary entries that describe his exciting observations through his telescope and his conflicts with the Church.
- T-Chart: Make a list of Galileo's discoveries on one side of the chart and list the views of the Inquisition on the other side.
- Song Writer: Create a song or poem about Galileo's conflict with the Church.
- Spin Doctor: Create a poster supporting the Inquisition in its effort to stamp out the heretical thinking of Galileo.
- Counter Spin: Create a poster that supports the free scientific inquiry of Galileo and against the doctrines of the Inquisition and the Church.
- Rumper Sticker: Create a rumper sticker for the horses used by the judges of the Inquisition.
- Front Page: In a team of four student editors, create a front-page edition of the *Enlightenment Times* newspaper focusing on Galileo's discoveries and on his subsequent trial by the Inquisition.
- ADV Historical Research: Using the resources in your library and on the Internet, look for other instances in history when powerful institutions (such as governments or religious organizations) attempted to repress or stamp out new ideas that were contrary to their beliefs or ways of thinking. What happened as a result of this repression of new ideas? When finished, report your findings to the class.
- ADV Historical Analysis: Using sources in your library, try to find out what made the Catholic Church so afraid of Galileo's discoveries. Be sure to report your findings to the class.

- ADV The Futurist: If Galileo were alive today, what constitutional rights would he have to protect him from the Inquisition?

5.9.2   The Cartesian Way (1637)

René Descartes (1596–1650) was the founder of modern scientific methodology. Descartes was tired of the philosophers around him endlessly debating and going nowhere. He wanted a system of thinking on which everybody would agree and with which progress could be made at achieving definite answers. Descartes came up with four steps of scientific reasoning in his *Discourse on Method* (1637):

1. Never accept anything as the truth.
2. Divide any question into many separate questions.
3. Begin with the most simple and proceed to the most complex questions.
4. Be confident that nothing essential has been omitted.

Reason, he said, can be trusted because it exists in each human and, through careful methods of observation, can guide us to the basic principles that create a better understanding of our human existence. Descartes, with his "Cartesian" method of scientific reasoning, split the European mind between the physical, observed world we can describe with reason and the mental feelings of intuition from which humans make many decisions (Hulme and Jordanova 1990, 187; Prigogine 1996, 183–189).

Note from the Future: This division of the mind between the rational and the intuitive by Descartes will have a profound effect on the world.

- Quick Write: Think of a problem you currently face. Write this problem down. Now, break this problem down into as many smaller questions as possible. Arrange these questions in order—simplest to more complex. (This is Cartesian thinking. State the problem, break it into parts, and proceed from the simple to the most complex in solving the problem.)
- Ace Reporters: As a team of four ace reporters of the *Enlightenment Times* newspaper, create a front-page edition on René Descartes and the importance of his scientific method.
- ADV Research: Compare Cartesian methods of doing research with other methods. Decide which method you think is best and defend your point of view.

5.9.3   The Enlightenment of Buddha

Across Asia, the European Enlightenment caused a great deal of puzzlement. Descartes, in Europe, taught that the world was divided between the physical, observable world, which could be studied and understood, separated from the mental, illogical world of intuition and feelings of the mind. This was the key of the European Enlightenment—but not of the Buddhist concept of Enlightenment. Rather than split the mind between the observable, physical world and the intuitive, mental world, the Buddhist goal of Enlightenment was to create one personal and unified understanding of the whole world—physical and mental—together at one time. A Cartesian scientist in the West would systematically record observations of a leaf to make rational conclusions about the leaf. A Buddhist seeking enlightenment, however, would sit down and meditate about the same leaf. The meditation would continue until the Buddhist could see beyond the physical properties of the leaf to realize that the physical properties are only part of a much larger whole—that is both mental and physical at the same time. This point of "being at one with the universe" is the Buddhist Enlightenment.

- Quick Write: Think back to a time when you just sat and watched a cloud pass by, the setting sun on a mountaintop, or the changing colors of a tree. Describe your experience in a short paragraph and share it with your class.
- Art Mart: Draw a picture of a cloud, a tree, or an ocean wave and try to visualize your drawing as part of the whole planet.
- T Chart: Using a T chart, compare the Cartesian and Buddhist views of the world.
- Meet the Press: You are in luck! Descartes and Buddha (two students in costume) are in town and have agreed to appear on your popular Enlightenment TV show. All the reporters (members of the class) should make a list of three to five questions to ask your guests.
- ADV Cultural Comparison: How can two cultures—such as Christian and Buddhist—on the same planet, have such completely different concepts of the world in which we live?
- ADV Futurist: Use your library and the Internet to try to find out why some scientists, 400 years after Descartes, are now moving away from Descartes and toward a more Buddhist view of the Earth as a whole entity?

5.9.4   Newton: The Majestic Clockwork (1687)

Galileo, after his trial by the Inquisition in 1632, predicted that the center of science and commerce would shift from Catholic Italy to Protestant northern Europe. He was right. By 1650, Protestant northern Europe dominated both science and commerce. One of the major scientific leaders in northern Europe was Isaac Newton (1642–1727). As a boy in England, he did not receive a very good education, but he loved mathematics. He was smart enough to graduate from Cambridge; during the plague years of 1665 and 1666, he stayed at home and on his own developed a new mathematical method of why things fluctuate—we now call it calculus. He was also curious why the moon never fell into the Earth, and he calculated that the moon falls so fast toward Earth that it constantly misses Earth and keeps going around it. From his studies of the moon—not the apple—he calculated his general law of gravity. He was also fascinated with light; through careful observation and calculation, he determined that the spectrum of colors formed in a rainbow or a lens is not accidental but is the set physical colors of all light in the universe. The impact this poor village lad had on the world was staggering. Suddenly, movements of waves could be calculated by his new math (calculus). The distance a cannonball could be shot could be calculated. Painters now had an understanding of light and could use colors more accurately. To Newton, the universe was a majestic mechanical clockwork run by mathematics (Bronowski 1973, 221–245).

- Quick Apple: Throw a ball high in the air to a friend and then describe in a short paragraph the arc the ball makes as it travels toward your friend.
- Catch a Wave: Watch a wave in a pond or tank of water and then describe the shape of the wave as it moves. Imagine and describe a giant tidal wave hitting the shore after a volcanic eruption. (Newton developed calculus to calculate the power of such waves.)
- Over the Rainbow: Describe a time you saw a rainbow and exactly what it looked like.
- Front Page Edition: In teams of four, develop a front-page edition of the *Enlightenment Times* newspaper describing all the discoveries of Isaac Newton. Be sure to include an interview with him and an illustration demonstrating one of his major discoveries.

- ADV Calculus Demo: Without getting too complicated, have a teacher or a senior high school student give a simple demonstration of how calculus works.
- ADV What If?: Without the discoveries of Isaac Newton, where would the world be today? Make a list of the things we could not do today if we did not have the discoveries of Newton.
- ADV Counter Spin: Develop an argument against Newton and the idea that the whole universe runs on mathematics.

5.10.0   INVENTION AND REVOLUTION

5.10.1   Agricultural Revolution

The Enlightenment reached England before it reached the rest of Europe. This was due, in part, to England being an island with a separate language and culture, which led to a national identity. It was also due to Henry VIII creating his own national Church of England during the Reformation, thereby breaking the religious, economic, and political power of the Catholic Church in England. It was also due to Cromwell's breaking the power of the king and the feudal system of nobles who controlled the land. The people of England were now freed from all their feudal obligations to the king, nobles, and Church—were beginning to experiment and think of ways to improve their lives. New types of thinking and doing things were beginning to pay off for the English people before the rest of Europe. Many of these new ways of thinking were in the area of agriculture: more former Church and royal lands were freed for growing crops, new and better seeds, rotation of crops, and better plows. The agricultural revolution was in the air in England and with it, the beginnings of the nineteenth century, while the rest of Europe was still trapped in the feudalism of the Middle Ages with its kings, nobles, and castles.

- Quick Write: Describe how you feel when you are able to eat better, wear better clothes, and have pride in earning your own money.
- Bumper Sticker: Create a bumper sticker supporting the agricultural revolution during the late eighteenth century.
- Poster Power: Create a poster illustrating the immense number of political, religious, and economic changes that were taking place in England.

- Quick Skit: With four partners, create a short skit that demonstrates the many changes taking place in England between 1600 and 1800.
- ADV Historical Research: Using your library, look for other instances of major changes in a country such as in England during the agricultural revolution. What were the results of these major changes? How did they change the country and its people? Report to the class on your findings.

5.11.0 ART AND CREATIVE THOUGHT

5.11.1 Descartes and the Music of the Spheres (circa 1618)

One of the major thinkers of the Enlightenment, Descartes, thought that everything could be explained by reason. Naturally, he tried to put music and reason together. He reasoned that the simpler and the more harmonic the music, the more mathematical it was. He quickly realized, however, that music needed dissonance that was not mathematical to make it enjoyable. He also noted that different individuals preferred different types of music. He quickly concluded that music was tied to the passions of humans rather than to mathematics and reason.

Musical Notes from the Future: Descartes' discovery during the Enlightenment that good music did not follow mathematical or rational models opened the door for the radical musical changes that took place with the romantic movement during the nineteenth century (Hulme and Jordanova 1990, 47–65).

- Quick Write: Write a short paragraph on why you enjoy music. Is what you experience in music more intellectual or more emotional?
- T Chart: Play a musical piece by Bach from the Enlightenment and compare it to a piece by Beethoven during the nineteenth century. Using the T chart, compare the two types of music. What differences can you hear? Share your observations with the class.
- Ace Reporter: As the ace reporter of the *Enlightenment Times* newspaper, interview Descartes (another fellow student) concerning his startling discovery that music did not fit into mathematical formulas and reasoning. Both the ace reporter and Descartes should then write up the interview for the next edition of the *Enlightenment Times*.

- ADV Biography: Read a biography of Descartes that describes his actual attempts to make music mathematical and reasonable. Report to the class on what insights you gained from the biography.

5.11.2   Shakespeare: Double, Double, Toil and Trouble (1603)

William Shakespeare (1564–1616) was not well educated. He made many mistakes in geography, history, and biblical references. He had no interest in science, and he borrowed heavily from other writers of his day. Despite these flaws, Shakespeare is considered the greatest writer and playwright of all time. How come?

He could WRITE! His words poured across the page with frolicsome abandon. His simple characters played havoc with the language and changed nouns to verbs, adjectives to verbs, and pronouns to nouns: "Hark, hark the lark at heaven's gate sings." His characters are vile (Richard III), thoughtful (Hamlet), and evil (Iago). He juggled disguises, shifted scenes, and created plays within plays. He was a philosopher equal to Descartes or Bacon but just as swiftly made fun of them. He was a royalist but made fun of kings. He was religious but made fun of religions. He also never published any of his plays. After his death, for no profit, friends of his published two hundred copies of *The First Folio* (1623), thirty-six of his plays bound together.

The Puritans hated Shakespeare—he made too much fun of religion and their strict rules. When the Puritans came to power in 1642, they closed all the theaters in England, ending one of the greatest periods of drama in history (Durant and Durant 1961, 87–109).

Note from the Future: The remaining copies of *The First Folio,* published in 1623, are today the most valuable nonreligious books in the world.

- Quick Write: How many rhyming words can you put into one sentence? (Shakespeare was a master at this kind of word play.)
- Pick a Play: In teams of four, pick a small part of one of Shakespeare's plays and read it as a team to the class with all the gusto of Shakespeare's day.
- Poster Power: Create a poster advertising one of Shakespeare's plays.
- Role Play: Role-play a stuffy Puritan very irate at Shakespeare's plays and present your impersonation to the class.
- Theater: Attend a Shakespeare play given locally and report on its production to the class.

- ADV Popularity Trend: Analyze how Shakespeare's plays written over 400 years ago in Elizabethan English can still be popular today.
- ADV Historical Analysis: Research in your library why certain cultural phenomena (such as "theater") rise to such greatness in a short period of time (such as Elizabethan England) and then are not repeated for hundreds, if not thousands, of years.

5.11.3   Cervantes: The Man of La Mancha

"Let this be your aim," said Miguel de Cervantes (1547–1616), "that by reading this story, melancholy be turned to laughter, and the cheerful man made merrier still." He was the world's first novelist and a man who faced innumerable hardships during his lifetime. His left hand was shot off. He was captured by the Turks. He was in debtors' prison. Out of these many trials came *Don Quixote,* the Man of La Mancha, the knight-errant of chivalry, with a rusty suit of armor, a decrepit horse named Rosinante, and a trusty sidekick named Sancho Panza. He fought to right wrongs and to defend his ladylove, Dulcinea. *Don Quixote* was in fact a common, middle-class hero dreaming of grandeur where rustic inns became castles, goat herders became gallant knights, and windmills became the feared giant enemy to battle. The world loved his story when it first hit the presses (1603), but typically, Cervantes had already sold the rights to his publisher for a small sum. Although Cervantes did not get the full financial benefit of his best-seller, *Don Quixote* was the first book written in Spanish, the first written for the common people rather than the nobles, and the first to look inward at the dreams and frailties of the human individual. He paved the way for the modern novel and the movie plots of the twentieth century. Ironically, this national hero of Spain died the same day as Shakespeare (April 23, 1616) and was buried in an unmarked grave near Madrid (Boorstin 1992, 298–308)

- Quick Write: Think of a favorite movie hero or heroine. Describe what makes this person special for you.
- Poster Power: Create a poster of Don Quixote and all the fabulous things he could do (in his mind).
- Rumper Sticker: Create a rumper sticker for the backside of Don Quixote's decrepit horse, Rosinante.

- Venn Diagram: Using a Venn diagram, compare the basic plot of Don Quixote with a typical movie plot of the late twentieth century. How are they similar and different from each other?
- Role Play: In teams of four, create a short skit based on the basic elements of Don Quixote put into a modern setting, and present it to the class.
- ADV Historical Research: From your library and the Internet, read more about Cervantes and his influence on modern novel writing and screenplays, and report your findings to the class.

5.11.4   Mozart: The Boy Wonder

Wolfgang Amadeus Mozart (1756–1791) from Salzburg, Austria, died at the age of thirty-six and was buried in a mass grave in Vienna. Although he did not live long, Mozart is still considered one of the greatest composers who ever lived. Haydn said of the young Mozart to his father: "Before God . . . your son is the greatest composer known to me either in person or by reputation" (Gay 1966, 127–129).

He gave harpsichord concerts at the age of six, toured Europe when he was eight, wrote his first opera when he was twelve, and composed some of the best music the world has ever known. Mozart's problem was that he never found a patron who would support his musical composing. He was constantly out of money and forced to write music for all sorts of people for little or no money. In Mozart lay the glory of the Enlightenment. His was some of the best music ever written, but he died poor, sick, and alone. The Enlightenment died a similar death in the blood of the French Revolution (Boorstin 1992, 448–451; Gay 1966, 127–129).

- Quick Write: Who is your favorite musician? Write a short paragraph describing your favorite musician.
- Ad Campaign: In teams of four, create an ad campaign to help Mozart find a sponsor for his music. Develop an advertising poster, a bumper sticker, and a thirty-second TV jingle to present to your class.
- Movie Time: Rent the movie *Amadeus* about the life of Mozart and give a report on it to the class.
- Eulogy: With a partner, compose a poem, rap, or song in memory of Mozart.

- ADV Historical Research: Look through history to find other brilliant young people who gave the world so much but died so young. Of these people, who do you think is the most important for his or her contribution to the world?
- ADV Brain Research: Recently, brain researchers have theorized that listening to Mozart makes humans think smarter. Locate information on this topic and report back to the class on your findings.

5.11.5   The Taj Mahal: For the Love of Mumtaz (1650)

The Mongul Empire in India (1526–1707) created some of the greatest art in the world during the Enlightenment. Emperor Akbar (1556–1605) consolidated Muslim control over northern India and celebrated his rule with an explosion of beautiful buildings, poetry, painting, and music. He was a Muslim foreigner and a Mongol descendent of Genghis Khan in a predominantly Hindu country. He was also the first to have a vision of a unified, national state of India. Heroically, he attempted to unite Christian, Muslim, and Hindu into one religion for India, but met with strong opposition. The unifying theme of his family's monumental artwork, however, can still be seen and heard across India today. Due to his influence, Muslim musicians still dominate Indian musical concerts today. The remains of his family's architectural works are also still considered some of the finest achievements in the world. The most famous is a national treasure of India—the Taj Mahal at Agra. Shah Jahan (1627–1658), Akbar's son, built the Taj Mahal in memory of his beautiful wife, Mumtaz. In a tragic irony of history, Shah Jahan was later imprisoned by his own son at Agra and he died gazing at the magnificent monument he built to his departed wife (Watson 1974, 108–118).

- Quick Draw: Make a sketch of what you think the most beautiful building in the world might look like.
- Song Writer: Create a song of Shah Jahan's love for Mumtaz.
- Map Attack: On a blank map of the world, locate India and Agra, the location of the Taj Mahal. How many miles is it from your hometown?
- Travel Brochure: Create a travel brochure advertising a trip to the Taj Mahal.
- Travel Rep: Have your company of four travel reps (students) plan a trip to Agra and the Taj Mahal. Call up an airline to find how much it would cost to fly to New Delhi, the capital of India. Agra is just

Illustration 5.11.5   *The Taj Mahal circa 1650, in Agra, India*

south of New Delhi. Estimate how much the whole trip, plus food and hotels, would cost.

- You Were There: As the host of this top TV program during the Enlightenment, have reporters (students) interview Akbar and all the religious leaders—Christian, Muslim, and Hindu—whom Akbar attempted to unite into one Indian religion. The reporters should concentrate on why this noble effort of Akbar's failed.

- ADV Futurist: Research why Hindus and Muslims are so bitterly opposed to each other in India and Pakistan today when they share the great artistic heritage of Akbar and his family.

5.12.0   SUCCESSES AND FAILURES OF THE ENLIGHTENMENT

5.12.1   Success or Failure?

This is the competitive quiz show that challenges teams to list as many reasons as possible why a person, place, or thing is the most important success or failure of the Enlightenment.

1. Each student team of four draws the name of an Enlightenment person, place, or thing from a hat.
2. Each team calls out its name and the scorekeeper puts it on the board as the team's name.
3. Using any books or materials available, each student team has fifteen minutes to make as long a list as possible of reasons why their chosen name is the most important of the era.
4. The Enlightenment names to be used can be as follows or developed from a larger list:

reason	Thirty Years War	Peter Paul Rubens
Cervantes	Shakespeare	Frankenstein
James Cook	scientific method	Rousseau
Mirabeau	Robespierre	Mozart
Akbar	Louis XIV	John Calvin
René Descartes	Inquisition	Galileo
Cromwell	absolute kings	Francis Bacon
nationalism	Immanuel Kant	Mother Earth

5. A scorekeeper will keep track of how many answers each team gives on the board.
6. The team with the most number of "valid" supporting reasons wins a free trip to the library.

5.13.0   MAJOR WORLD PROBLEMS FOR THE ENLIGHTENMENT

5.13.1   The Dark Side of the Enlightenment

In many ways, the crowning achievement of the Enlightenment was at the same moment its downfall—*The Declaration of the Rights of Man* (1789) during the French Revolution:

1. The declaration says that each individual is born free and equal—following John Locke's ideas of individual freedom.
2. The declaration says that, if the citizens of a nation-state participate in governing, that country has the power to make the rules for everybody in the state—following Rousseau's concept of Social Contract.

Together, these ideas from the *Declaration of the Rights of Man* produce the fundamental ideals of the national state in which individual citizens have the right, the freedom, and the duty to make their own laws. It is a document against unjust governments everywhere—even in the twenty-first century. But it has two dark sides:

1. What happens to minorities in a nation-state who are excluded from being citizens? They are given no protection of freedom and equality against the laws produced by the recognized "citizens" of the state.
2. What happens to neighboring nation-states that have their own idea of "citizenship"—separate from and outside the laws developed by the citizens of "our" nation-state? Two nation-states, in this dark side of the Enlightenment, can go to war and fight over what each considers to be theirs.

Three Notes from the Future:

1. Nation-states during the nineteenth and twentieth centuries justified their discrimination and committed genocide against peoples of different colors, ethnicities, and religion based on the concept that they were not "citizens" of their nation-state.
2. Wars between nation-states during the nineteenth and twentieth centuries were justified because the "citizens" of one state wanted something in another state.
3. Karl Marx, during the nineteenth century, viewed the Enlightenment and the *Declaration of the Rights of Man* as a manifesto of the rising middle class imposing its will on the common workers who were not politically literate enough to be participating citizens in the state (see Hulme and Jordanova 1990, 186–199).

- Quick Write: From your own point of view, describe in a short paragraph why certain people are discriminated against.
- T Chart: On one side of the T chart, describe the positive ideals of the *Declaration of the Rights of Man,* and on the other side, the negative results of these ideals.
- Poster Power: Create a poster that illustrates both the positive and negative aspects of the *Declaration of the Rights of Man*.
- Newspaper Editor: In teams of four, create a front-page edition of the *Enlightenment Times* newspaper that exposes the *Declaration of the Rights of Man* to many different points of view.

- ADV Historical Viewpoints: Research the following events and peoples in terms of the principles of the *Declaration of the Rights of Man*:
  1. The treatment of the American Indian and African Americans in nineteenth- and twentieth-century United States.
  2. The treatment of Jews in nineteenth- and twentieth-century Europe.
  3. The treatment of factory workers in nineteenth-century Europe.
  4. Military alliances and wars between nation-states, such as during World War I, in the twentieth century.

5.14.0   ENLIGHTENMENT ANTECEDENTS FOR THE FUTURE

5.14.1   The End of Reason?

Physically, the end of the Enlightenment came violently with the French Revolution. All reason was forgotten as the heads of the French nobility were chopped off. The intellectual end of the Enlightenment, however, came from two sources in Germany. The first was Immanuel Kant (1724–1804). Kant openly questioned the center of Enlightenment thinking in his book *Critique of Pure Reason* (1781): Do humans really follow reason when they make decisions? People can make careful scientific observations following exact scientific methods, said Kant, but can they ever be sure they have made enough observations to be absolutely sure they understand what is happening? People have different backgrounds and different experiences. Two different observers, due to their backgrounds, can see very different things. In the end, says Kant, a person must make a decision not based on endless scientific observations, but on an educated guess as to which decision to make. Kant called this final part of decision making "a leap of faith."

The second intellectual end to the Enlightenment (*Aufklarung*) also came from Germany in the form of a reactionary movement called the "Force and Violence" (*Sturm und Drang*). The members of this movement wanted a national German state, not a mass of small city-states. In their call for a national state, they strongly opposed "foreign" ideas, such as the Enlightenment from France and England. They also opposed the major idea of the Enlightenment—reason. They wanted Germans to live according to their own feelings and emotions—love, hate, anger, and joy. It was the formal intellectual end of the Enlightenment and the beginning of the romantic movement that swept across Europe during the early nineteenth century (Gay 1966, 146–147).

- Quick Watch: As a class, watch a short, complex scene from a famous movie. Now, individually, write a paragraph about what happened in the scene. As a class, compare the observations of each student by charting how many students saw different things in the scene. How many students had the same understanding of what happened in the scene? How many different views of what happened are there in the class? (The differences between what is seen represent Kant's major argument for fully *not* trusting reason and observation.)
- Bumper Sticker: Create a bumper sticker that supports either the Enlightenment, Kant, or Sturm und Drang.
- ADV Time Traveler: Go back to the Enlightenment and interview Descartes, Kant, and the Sturm und Drang leaders (students in character) to compare their ways of thinking. How are they different from each other?
- ADV Poster Power: Create a poster that compares the thinking of Descartes, Kant, and the Sturm und Drang leaders about the power of reasoning.
- ADV Futurist #1: Using resources in your library and on the Internet, travel forward to the nineteenth century to analyze the influence the Sturm und Drang movement had on the romantic movement.
- ADV Futurist #2: Using sources in your library and on the Internet, travel forward to the twentieth century to examine the influence of the Sturm und Drang movement on the development of Hitler and the Nazi Party before World War II in Germany.

5.14.2 Is Humankind Ready to Advance?

It is now time to judge whether or not humankind is ready to advance into the next era:

- Five members from around Enlightenment Town (the class) will state their basic viewpoints of whether or not enough advances have been made during the Enlightenment. The five illustrious members are as follows:
  1. LeDuc de Betron, the archconservative of Enlightenment Town, who believes that humankind has gone far enough with enough

progress. Betron believes strongly that the good old days were the best and that humankind needs to hold strongly to past values and beliefs.

2. Ruban Derudzuk, one of the rising young voices in the town, is a more moderate conservative who believes that we need to be very cautious with any change and be very sure that no harm will come to Enlightenment Town if change takes place. Ruban is willing to accept some change, but only in very small amounts and only when the time is right—and wants to decide when that time will come.

3. Louie Wookbot, the wishy-washy middle-of-the-roader around town, is willing to accept change for a few minutes after one speaker, but may have a change of mind in an instant to oppose change after another speaker has finished.

4. Descartes Vatsmeer, the moderate progressive of the group is willing to support change for the good of the people in Enlightenment Town. Vatsmeer is especially in favor of changes that will directly benefit Vatsmeer's own family.

5. Robespierre Varull, the radical progressive of the town, is very willing to support any change that will move humanity away from a drafty and leaky basement apartment into something more modern and comfortable for humanity.

- Each member of Enlightenment Town (classroom) now must chose one of the five positions for humanity to take and must support the position with evidence of what he or she has learned about the Enlightenment.

- A vote will then be taken of all commoners and nobles around town to determine whether or not humanity should move on to the next era. The consensus decision of the imaginary citizens of Enlightenment Town will determine their own future and the rest of humanity. (In reality, such decisions by people during the Enlightenment were key in deciding whether humans stayed the way they were or progressed to new levels of development.)

The Nineteenth Century (1800 to 1899)

UNIT 6: TABLE OF CONTENTS

INTRODUCTION TO THE NINETEENTH CENTURY

"Man is born free, yet everywhere he is in chains!" wrote Rousseau in *Social Contract* (1762), during the height of the Enlightenment. These chains that bind human freedom are the story of the nineteenth century. Freedom of thought for the individual protected by the new national state is the major idea that passed from the Enlightenment of the eighteenth century to the age of industrialization and imperialism of the nineteenth century. This individualism was expressed in the romantic artistic expression of the music of Beethoven, the poetry of Byron, and the paintings of David. This individualism of the Enlightenment, however, clashes head-on with the dominant forces of the nineteenth century—industrialization, nationalism, and colonialism. Industrialism tied the individual to the new factories across Europe. Nationalism did the same to the aims of the new nation-states. Colonialism also tied the individual to the expansion of the new industrial nations of Europe. The reaction to these three forces was a major theme of the century. Karl Marx sought to have the workers, not the capitalists, control the factories. Charles Dickens wrote sympathetically about the plight of the workers in the factories. Claude Monet's impressionist paintings, with swirls of light and color, muted the ugliness of the age of factories. Nietzsche wrote passionately for each individual to realize that the economic, social, and religious "worlds" they created around them also chained them to their creations. His powerful call for the "will to power" of the individual carried deep into the following twentieth century.

THEMATIC LESSON PACS FOR THE NINETEENTH CENTURY

6.1.0 HISTORICAL TIME LINE

6.1.1 Nineteenth-Century History Time Line

- Name Plates: Photocopy six sets of the fourteen names and items below. Cut each name or item into a strip of paper. Place the strips of paper carefully into separate envelopes for each team and label the envelopes "6.1.1 The Nineteenth-Century History Time Line" for later use in class.

- Group Power: Break the class into six teams.
- The Envelope: Each team should be given an envelope containing the following random fourteen names from the nineteenth century:
  1. First English railway completed (1830)
  2. Berlin Conference under Bismarck divided Africa (1884)
  3. Turner created impressionist painting (1829)
  4. The Congress of Vienna divided Europe (1815)
  5. England abolished the slave trade (1807)
  6. Beethoven died (1820)
  7. Napoleon crowned emperor of France (1804)
  8. Marx wrote the *Communist Manifesto* (1848)
  9. Darwin published *Origin of the Species* (1859)
  10. Kingdom of Italy established (1860)
  11. Radium discovered by Marie Curie (1898)
  12. Perry opened Japan (1853)
  13. Suez Canal opened (1863)
  14. Dostoevsky published *Crime and Punishment* (1866)
- Team Time Line: The first job of each team is to correctly order the fourteen names and artifacts according to time, with the oldest at the top and the most recent at the bottom. Each student should separately write the correct time line for the nineteenth-century names and artifacts on a personal sheet of paper for later reference.
- Team Look Up: Once the members of the team have their own nineteenth-century time lines on their own sheets of paper, each of the fourteen nineteenth-century names should be divided between members of the team to find out the meaning of each name from the textbook. Once found, the meanings of each nineteenth-century name can be shared with the members of their team to write on their own time lines.
- Poster Power: On a large piece of paper, each team should construct its own time line for the nineteenth century using the fourteen names with descriptions and illustrations to demonstrate the meaning of each name. When finished, these can be presented to the class and displayed on the classroom wall.
- Music Mart: Each team should pick what they think is the most important name or event in the time line and then compose a short song or rap about the name or event. When finished, this can be presented to the class for their approval.

• Journal Entry: Have each team member write a short journal entry speculating about what he or she now knows about the development of humans during the nineteenth century and possibly the most important things to happen during this era. When finished, students can first share their thoughts with their team and then with the class as a whole for general discussion about what they think are the most important things that happened during the era.

6.1.2   An End-of-Unit History Chain for the Industrial Age

A fun way to conduct an end-of-unit review for assessment is to create a class history chain. The steps to conduct a history chain are as follows:

1. The teacher should place each of the major names (without years attached) mentioned in the unit on an 8½"-x-11" sheet of paper using a minimum of a 72-point typeface so that everyone can read the name across the room. These names on paper should be collected at the end of the lesson and stored in a folder for multiple use.
2. To begin the lesson, each student should stand and come to the front of the room and randomly be given one of the names. The students should then hold the names in front of them—facing outward—so that everybody in class can see the name.
3. The students should now make themselves into a nineteenth-century history chain by having the student with the oldest name, event, or thing at one far corner of the room and then placing themselves in chronological order across the front of the room to the most recent name, event, or thing in another corner of the room. (Expect fun chaos as students talk to each other and determine—by themselves—their own chronological order.)
4. Once the nineteenth-century history chain across the room has been established, the teacher can then review the chain by having each student identify their name, event, or thing and its relative place in the time line. (The teacher can expect to have more than a few corrections to make as students describe their name and the place of each in history—but remember, this is an excellent and fun way to review.)
5. As a second step in the history chain, the teacher should group the students into teams of about six students each, to have each team

determine which is the most important name in their part of the chain for its impact on the world.

6. The teacher then should collect all the history chain name papers and save them to be used later. Students may then take their seats.

7. In a short journal entry, each student should then record what he or she thinks are the three most important things that happened in the era and then share them with the class to generate a full-class consensus on the meaning of the era.

6.2.0   SEPARATING FACT FROM MYTH AND PROPAGANDA

6.2.1   The Nineteenth-Century Romantic

During the early nineteenth century, in one of the first times in history, an individual human could express the deepest personal emotions of joy, sorrow, anger, or love—and then go out and live according to his emotions. They called it romanticism and its foremost practitioner was the English poet Lord Byron (1788–1824). Just before his death at age thirty-six, he wrote:

Tred those reviving passions down,
Unworthy manhood!—unto thee
Indifferent should the smile or frown
Of Beauty be.
If thou regret'st thy youth, why live?
The land of honorable death
Is here:—up to the Field, and give
Away thy breath.

All of England mourned his passing. He was a dashing young poet who lived his life to the fullest, who said what he thought, and did whatever he wanted. The ancient Greeks of Aristotle and Socrates times had been dead for thousands of years but Byron, true to his romantic ideals, wrote endlessly of the glories of ancient Greece and how ancient Greece should rise again. He inspired the Greek nationalists to rebel against the Turks and inspired many in England and Europe to support their fight. He died for a cause in which he believed (Palmer 1974, 72–79)

- Quick Write: In a short paragraph, express your feelings on something you love or hate and share this "romantic" expression with your class.

- T Chart: With a partner, use a T chart to think about the advantages and disadvantages of everybody saying exactly what they thought and doing exactly what they wanted.
- Rumper Sticker: Create a romantic rumper sticker Lord Byron could use on his horse.
- Poster Power: Create a poster that illustrates the romantic ideals of Lord Byron in his fight for independence for the Greek nation.
- Counter Spin: In a team of four, create a short skit that illustrates the dangers of romanticism, with four individuals with very strange "ideals." The class should then discuss why such romantic views could be dangerous. How should people with such views be handled?
  1. A man who wants to blow up the world and move to Mars
  2. A lady who wants taxpayers to pay to send all pigeons to Australia
  3. A man who believes aliens in black helicopters are invading the United States
  4. A lady who believes that the world is coming to an end tomorrow
- ADV Historical Analysis: Research the library and the Internet to find sources that compare the development of individualism, romanticism, and nationalism during the nineteenth century. When finished, present your findings to your class.

6.2.2   The Nineteenth-Century Origins of Nationalism and Patriotism

Although the Enlightenment encouraged individual reason, the romantic movement of the late eighteenth and early nineteenth centuries encouraged demonstrations of feelings, such as love, hate, and valor. One branch of this romanticism turned toward the feelings of national identity—especially in areas that had no national state, such as Germany, Italy, and Greece. Nationalists during the nineteenth century were always intellectuals from the cities of Europe who claimed the superiority of rural peasant virtues of a particular ethnic and language group. Ironically, the real peasants in these areas had little or no interest in "nationalism" of the romantic city intellectuals. German nationalists claimed that they had the virtue and power to make their "place in the sun." French nationalists believed they had the duty to civilize the world. The British regarded themselves as superior and that all others were "lesser breeds." The nationalists of the United States believed that they were "God's own country." Such feelings were purposely encouraged by politicians to tie the common people to a specific ethnic and language group and created genuine new national states in such areas as Germany and Italy. Such feelings of national and ethnic identity also created a great deal of bloodshed between different nations and ethnic groups during the coming twentieth century (Stambrook 1969).

- Quick Write: In a short paragraph, describe your feelings toward your own national state (for example, the United States) and how these feelings influence your views toward other countries.
- Bumper Sticker: Create a bumper sticker supporting the creation of one of the new national states—Germany, Italy, or Greece—during the nineteenth century.
- Poster Power: Create a poster that reflects the nationalistic feelings of patriotism in Germany, Italy, or Greece.
- Music Mart: Create a nationalistic song or rap that glorifies a single nation or ethnic group.
- Viewpoints: In teams of four, pick a country and then present different views of nationalism and patriotism in that country from a diehard patriot, a scared young soldier going to fight in one of his country's wars, a recent immigrant facing discrimination from the country's nationalists, and an international traveler who does not believe in national patriotism.
- T Chart: With a partner, create a T chart that illustrates the positives and negatives of nationalism and patriotism.
- ADV Futurist #1: Research your library for a list of all the wars and conflicts that have been fought during the nineteenth and twentieth centuries for the causes of nationalism and patriotism.
- ADV Futurist #2: In groups of four, discuss what alternatives there are to nationalism and ethnic identity and if such alternatives could work in the future.

6.2.3   Scientific Racism during the Nineteenth Century

The nineteenth century was an age of science. Ever since the time of Descartes and Newton in the Enlightenment, European scholars began to place everything into rational and objective scientific categories that, they believed, lay within an understandable universe based on mathematics and science. For much of the observable world, such categories worked and resulted in many of the advancements in the agricultural and industrial revolutions. What these thinkers of the nineteenth century did not realize, however, was that many things in our universe cannot be placed in scientific categories and that not everything can be viewed or stated in purely objective terms. Some scholars tried to "scientifically" categorize personalities and intelligence by facial expressions. Some scholars attempted to "scientifically" measure intelligence by skull size. Other scholars, such as Blumbach, (see TLP 5.5.2) attempted to classify the beauty of skulls by ethnic groups. European scholars conducted all of these studies during the eighteenth and nineteenth centuries, in an age when Europe was seeking to dominate the world with the products of its industrial revolution and its Christian religion. Consciously or unconsciously, all of the studies by European scholars of other ethnic groups concluded that Europeans were superior—by every measurement. Such studies added support to the belief that it was the right and duty of Europe to "civilize" (Europeanize) the rest of the world. Such studies comparing different ethnic groups were accepted as the truth because they were "scientific," regardless of the European bias or prejudice that lay behind the study. Today, we recognize this as "scientific racism"—the attempt to support ethnic bias and prejudice with scientific methods. Europeans and Americans during the nineteenth and twentieth centuries, as a result of this "scientific racism," could feel that they were superior to other ethnic groups because there was "scientific" evidence of this. Such "scientific racism" by Europeans and Americans during the nineteenth century led to such actions as the elimination of the American Indian in many parts of the United States, the wholesale killing of the Maori in New Zealand, and the continued enslavement of Africans (Pahl 1997).

- Quick Write: In a short paragraph, describe why you think your eye color is superior to all other eye colors. What if everything you did during your life depended upon your eye color?
- Simulated Racism: Divide your class according to eye color—brown eyes in one corner, blue eyes in another corner. Have each eye color group create an imaginary set of laws favor their eye color in such areas of academic grades, entrance to college, and job salary. Each group should then share their hypothetical laws with the whole class. What would happen if such laws were real? Are such laws in existence for different ethnic groups?
- Music Mart: Create a song or a rap that describes the scientific racism by the Europeans and Americans during the nineteenth and twentieth centuries.

- Front Page: In editorial teams of four students each, create a front-page edition for the *Industrial Times* newspaper that describes the scientific racism of the nineteenth and twentieth centuries. Be sure to include interviews with members of different ethnic groups affected by the racism.
- You Were There: As the host of this popular nineteenth-century TV show, have the members of your studio audience each write three questions to ask each of your guests today about the scientific racism of the nineteenth and twentieth centuries. Your four guests (students in costume) are as follows:
  1. Sir/Lady Budlong Erk—a diehard colonialist who believes that it is the right and duty of the Europeans to civilize all of the other peoples in the world
  2. Madine Deron—the very last Maori in New Zealand still alive
  3. Baritl Portan—a Cormoro Islander who fears the island will be conquered by the Europeans in the near future
  4. Evline LaPure—the spouse of a Christian missionary
- ADV The Futurist: Conduct an analysis to determine what influence "scientific racism" had on current laws and social and economic patterns in your community.

6.3.0   LOCATION AND MOVEMENT

6.3.1   Why Did England Take the Lead in the Industrial Revolution?

A multitude of factors enabled England to quickly take the lead in the industrial revolution of the nineteenth century, before the rest of Europe:

1. The English revolutions against the feudalism and the power of the nobles had started in 1641 with Oliver Cromwell—not in 1789, as in France.
2. The English revolutions freed up former feudal land that could be used for growing more grain and sheep to produce an agricultural revolution.
3. The agricultural revolution, in England, produced more food at a cheaper price.
4. The agricultural revolution freed many former farmers to work in the city factories.

5. The British Isles were blessed with rich supplies of iron and coal within a very short distance of each other.
6. The English invested heavily in developing a good road and transportation system—by road, canal, and then rail.
7. British merchants, since the 1600s, had made huge profits in the international trade of sugar, tea, tobacco, cotton, and slaves. They used their profits to invest in such new inventions as iron plows, steamships, coal and iron mines, textile factories, and railways.
8. Britain's large colonial empire provided raw materials, such as cotton and sugar, in return for the manufactured cloth and iron tools from England's factories—at a huge profit for England's merchants.
9. The British government created policies that encouraged industrial growth, lifted restrictions on foreign trade, stimulated canal and road construction, and provided for a strong navy to protect British merchant ships (Palmer 1974, 36–37).

- Quick Write: Think back for a moment to the proudest moment in your life. Write a short paragraph describing what made you so proud and what were the steps you took before that moment that made you so proud?
- Poster Power: Create a large poster for your classroom wall illustrating the many steps that led to the development of the industrial revolution in England.
- Bumper Sticker: Create a bumper sticker that promotes the development of the industrial revolution in England.
- Map Attack: Using a blank map of England, illustrate the different things that happened both coming into England and leaving England and that promoted the development of the industrial revolution in England.
- Role Play: In teams of four, role-play different people during the industrial revolution who assisted in making it successful in England:
  1. Jethro Armstrong—a canal builder
  2. Reginald Longbrow—a British government official
  3. Smedley Bolweaval—a cotton merchant from a southern state in the United States
  4. Jimmy Duster—a coal miner
  5. C. W. Baggs—a rich investor in the industrial revolution
- ADV Historical Analysis: Analyze the major contributing factors that led to the success of the industrial revolution in England and rank

these factors in terms of the order of importance. Make sure to state your reasons for the order of your selection.

6.3.2   Returning to Africa—Sierra Leone and Liberia

In 1772, slavery officially came to an end in England when Lord Mansfield declared that it was illegal under British common law. Between 1600 and 1800, upwards of five million Africans had been forcibly taken from their homes in West Africa by the Europeans and made to work without pay or freedom in America. That strange American Revolution of 1776 based on "liberty, freedom, and equality" did not include enslaved Africans in its "Declaration of Independence" from England. England quickly took note of this deliberate exclusion by the American colonists. As a result, throughout the American War of Independence, England offered freedom to any African slave who could reach the safety of British lines during the war. Although England eventually lost the war, thousands of former slaves from Africa fled from their American slave owners for the freedom of British rule during the American Revolution. These freed American slaves, at first, settled in Arcadia, Nova Scotia (in Canada), and then moved to Sierra Leone in West Africa in 1792. Sierra Leone was initially set up in 1787 as a colony for freed African slaves by the British government. Freed African Americans set up neighboring Liberia in 1815 on their own. Sierra Leone, however, served several more purposes for the British than just returning Africans to Africa. Most of the Africans who first settled Sierra Leone could speak English well, wore Western clothing, could read and write well, and were Christian. England saw these "new Africans" of Sierra Leone as agents in their imperial plans to "civilize" (control) large parts of Africa. The first secondary school and teacher's college in West Africa were established in Sierra Leone, as well as some of the first Christian missionary churches in Africa. These former American slaves became some of the first Christian missionaries in Africa. They also became some of the first merchants carrying European products to Africa, some of the first teachers in European schools across Africa, and some of the first administrators when England began to formally create a colonial empire in Africa later in the nineteenth century. By the end of the American Civil War in 1865, however, very few African Americans had actually returned to Africa. With the promise of freedom in the United States, most African Americans chose to stay in their new homeland—America (Ajayi and Espie 1965, 327–340).

Note from the Future: Throughout the nineteenth and most of the twentieth centuries, freed African American slaves and their descendants dominated the traditional African people in Sierra Leone and Liberia with European and American weapons, ideas, and religion. This role was reversed in the late twentieth century when the African American ruling elites in Sierra Leone and Liberia were removed from power by traditional African forces.

- Quick Write: Have you ever gone back to a place where you used to live? In a short paragraph, describe what it felt like returning to your old home. Did you get to see any old friends? Would you prefer to live at your former home, or at your present home with your family and friends?
- Map It: On a blank map of the world, trace the route of West Africans being enslaved and shipped to the United States, and then follow their return first to Canada and then to Sierra Leone and Liberia during the early nineteenth century.
- Poet's Corner: Create a poem expressing your feelings as a freed African slave returning to Africa.
- Your Choice: As a freed African American in 1820, with all your family and friends in the United States, would you chose to immigrate to either Sierra Leone or Liberia in Africa because Africans are your ancestors and have dark skin? Or would you decide to remain in the United States? State the reasons for your decision and share them with your class
- Poster Power: Create a poster that illustrates how the British used the freed African Americans in Sierra Leone in their mission to "civilize" (control) Africa.
- Role Play #1: In a team of four, create a short skit that illustrates the dilemma of the African Americans deciding whether to stay in the United States or immigrate to Africa.
- Role Play #2: In a team of four, create a short skit that illustrates the feelings of the traditional people of a country (Sierra Leone and Liberia) when a group of foreigners (African Americans) comes and tries to dominate their countries.
- ADV Historical Research: Research your library for evidence that the push for independence in the United States in 1776 was, in part,

a negative reaction against the abolition of the slave trade in England by Lord Mansfield in 1772.

- ADV The Futurist: Research the history of Sierra Leone and Liberia during the late twentieth century and investigate what happened to the former African Americans living there.
- ADV Historical Analysis: Use your library to conduct research on why returning to Africa was not very popular among African Americans during the nineteenth century, but was encouraged by former European American slave owners.

6.3.3   The Celestial Empire of China

For more than a thousand years, the Chinese "Mandate from Heaven" proclaimed that their society was superior to all other "barbarians." The Chinese government and people believed they had everything they needed to be a happy society, guided by duties for everyone as prescribed by Confucius. As late as the end of the eighteenth century and the beginning of the nineteenth, the Celestial Empire of China had successfully closed itself off to almost the entire outside world. The whole history of China had been one of successive land invasions, but with the Great Wall in place and successful diplomacy with its land-based neighbors, China could now feel secure and superior to all of the "barbarians" outside of China. But the world was changing. New food crops from the Americas (maize, sweet potatoes, and peanuts) were now major staples in the Chinese diet, and could be grown on marginal land. The result was a major population boom through the eighteenth and nineteenth centuries.

China, throughout its history, had defended itself against land invasions. Steeped in tradition and unwilling to rapidly change, the Celestial Empire of China was completely caught off guard when the Europeans began their gunboat diplomacy to force China to open its ports. All their thousand years of tradition did not prepare them for the European "barbarians" coming by sea.

During the last years of the Chinese Celestial Empire, the Manchu emperor Ch'ien-lung wrote the following words to His Majesty King George III of England in 1793:

Our Celestial Empire possesses all things in prolific abundance and lacks no product within its own borders. There was therefore no need to import the manufactures of outside barbarians in exchange for our own produce. But as the tea, silk and porcelain which the Celestial Empire produces, are absolute necessities to European nations and to yourselves, we have permitted as a signal mark of favor, that foreign trading houses be established at Canton, so that your wants might be supplied and your country thus participate in our beneficence. (Michael 1986, 170)

- Quick Write: From your experience, what are the dangers of relying on the traditional way of doing things and not being willing to change your ideas? Write a brief paragraph on your thoughts about this subject.
- Bumper Sticker #1: Create a bumper sticker King George III of England might like to stick on the throne of Chinese Emperor Ch'ien-lung.
- Bumper Sticker #2: Create a bumper sticker Chinese Emperor Ch'ien-lung might like to stick on the throne of King George III of England.
- Role Play #1: In a team of four, create a short role-play of the Chinese royal court writing the above letter to King George of England.
- Role Play #2: In a team of four, create a short role-play of the royal court of King George III of England writing a reply to the above letter from Chinese Emperor Ch'ien-lung.
- T Chart: Create a T chart that illustrates the differences between the thinking of the Chinese and the British at the start of the nineteenth century.
- Poster Power: Create a poster that illustrates the differences in thinking between the British and the Chinese at the beginning of the nineteenth century.
- ADV Historical Analysis #1: Research your library for other examples of countries that thought they were the best in the world and had nothing to learn from others. What happened to these countries?
- ADV Historical Analysis #2: Research your library for information on how China became so isolated in its history and came to view itself superior to all the other "barbarian" peoples of the world.
- ADV What If?: What if you were the major advisor to the emperor of China at the beginning of the nineteenth century? Would you advise a stronger isolation from the other countries of the world, or would you advise a rapid modernization to meet the growing threat from Europe?

6.3.4   A Canal at Suez (1869)

Suez is one of the most strategic places in the world. More ships pass through Suez today than almost any other place on Earth. The continents of Africa and Asia meet at Suez, the Mediterranean Sea and the Red Sea/Indian Ocean meet at Suez, and the most ancient civilizations—ancient Egypt, Assyria, and Mesopotamia—met at Suez. The ancient Egyptians dug a canal between the Red Sea and the Nile River in 700 B.C.E. to connect the Indian Ocean with the Mediterranean Sea. It remained a working canal for a thousand years, but as with most other things, it fell into disrepair during the early Middle Ages. Ferdinand-Marie de Lesseps revived the dream of creating a new canal across the Isthmus of Suez during the mid-nineteenth century. The advantage of such a canal was obvious—it would cut 6,000 miles off a trip between England and India around the Cape of Good Hope. De Lesseps was a visionary capitalist who wanted to create a canal that everybody in the world could own together. He offered shares in his canal-building company to the major countries in the world so everybody would share the Suez Canal peacefully. The United States was suspicious of any international organization that was not controlled by the United States and declined to purchase any shares. England thought that de Lesseps was part of a French plot to capture Egypt and did not purchase any shares. Many small individual investors from France, however, together with the ruler of Egypt, invested in the company and enabled de Lesseps to complete the canal in 1869. The canal was an immediate success—despite the suspicions of the United States and England. De Lesseps' company became the first large capitalistic company in the history of the world, with many small investors contributing to and then benefiting from the tremendous success of the canal. The world suddenly became a little bit smaller (Burchell 1966, 52–53).

- Quick Write: Think of a great moneymaking idea—an honest idea. Come up with the name of a company that could produce and sell this idea. Plan how to sell shares in your company so you can implement your plans.
- Map Attack: On a blank map of the world, locate the following:
  1. The meeting place of the continents of Asia and Africa
  2. The meeting place of the Mediterranean Sea and the Red Sea
  3. The Isthmus of Suez in modern Egypt

4. The old route from England to India around the Cape of Good Hope
5. The new route from England to India through the Suez Canal
- Stern Sticker: Create a stern sticker for the backsides of ships to advertise de Lesseps' new canal at Suez in 1869.
- Poster Power: Create a poster that illustrates the advantages of the Suez Canal over the old route to India around Africa.
- Madison Avenue: Create an ad campaign to sell shares in de Lesseps's Suez Canal Company. Be sure to include a radio jingle, a thirty-second TV spot, and an endorsement by a ship's captain.
- Washington Lobbyist: As a Washington lobbyist for de Lesseps, write a critical letter to a senator in Washington who did not support the building of the Suez Canal.
- ADV Historical Comparison: Using your library for research, compare the building of the Suez Canal with the building of the Panama Canal. What were the similarities and differences between the two projects? Report to the class on your findings.
- ADV The Futurist: Because the Panama Canal is getting too small for the number and the size of ships that pass through it, the United States is planning to build a canal across Nicaragua in the future. Your company (a team of four students) has been hired to develop the preliminary plans for building this canal. Prepare a set of plans for the canal and be sure to include a map of your proposed canal route, the depth and width of the canal for today's biggest ships, how many people you would like to hire for the project, its proposed cost, how many shares of stock you will sell to pay for it, and how long you think it will take you to build it.

6.3.5   European Imperialism

Lenin, during the early years of the twentieth century, saw "imperialism" (the expansion of an industrial country to get new markets for its goods) as the last stage of capitalism. Europe in the early 1800s was ready for imperialism. The agricultural revolution was producing more than enough food to feed all the people of Europe. As a result, the populations of Europe were beginning to explode and create new European settlements in "European colonies" in Africa, Asia, and the Americas. The inventions of the industrial revolution were also producing a surplus of cheap factory goods, such as textiles, iron tools, and weapons, ready to sell to other countries. At the same time, a Christian revival in Europe produced a strong call for Europeans to travel across the world to convert the "heathen" to Christianity (see also TLP 6.6.1 Missionary

Movement). Quite often, all three forces for Europe's imperial expansion took place at exactly the same time. Ships with new European settlers would also have European goods to sell and missionaries to convert people, all on the same boat. Europeans, as well as the peoples of Africa and Asia who were the major objects of this imperialism, quite often confused these three motives for imperialism. The European settlers were quite often the same people who sold the surplus textiles, iron tools, and weapons to the people of Africa and Asia. The same settlers and merchants in Africa and Asia were often also the Christian missionaries to the same countries. At the end of the nineteenth century, Rudyard Kipling jokingly called the European desire for imperialism to be "the White Man's burden"—the desire to recreate all the rest of the world in the image of Europe (Burchell 1966, 104–105).

- Quick Write: In a short paragraph, describe a time in your life when you did something for more than just one reason and then share this incident with the class.
- Poster Power: On a large poster, illustrate the three different aspects of European imperialism—settlers, exports, and missionaries.
- Protestor: As an African or Asian protestor during the time of European imperialism, create a song, poem, or slogan in opposition to the Europeans.
- Role Play: In a team of four, create a short skit in which a European settler, a European trader, and a European missionary all at the same time are trying to make a poor African into a European.
- Front Page: As the editorial team (of four students) for the *Industrial Times* newspaper, create a special front-page edition on European imperialism. Be sure to include an editorial on European imperialism and interview people with different views concerning imperialism.
- ADV The Futurist: Research the results of European imperialism. Focus especially on the people in the African and Asian colonies of Europe who begin to break free from European domination during the middle of the twentieth century.

6.4.0 POLITICS AND LEADERSHIP

6.4.1 The Congress of Vienna (1815)

There were high hopes when the leaders of Europe met in Vienna in 1814 to decide how Europe should be organized. Most of the nobility of Europe were there, including the czar of Russia, the king of Prussia, the emperor of Austria, Prince Talleyrand of France, Prince Metternich of Austria, and 16,000 secretaries, aides, horsemen, hairdressers, and pickpockets. Napoleon was defeated, his empire had collapsed, and large parts Europe—including France and Germany—were without any rulers (see also TLP 6.7.2 Lieutenant Napoleon Bonaparte). The congress was to decide how to organize a peaceful Europe after the many conquests and wars of Napoleon, but most of the congress was a façade. In reality, it met for only one day; everything had been decided in small backroom dealings. Only nobles officially attended the congress, and they had little interest in such things as new nations and representative forms of government. They wanted to return Europe to before the French Revolution of 1789. As a result, these nobles in Vienna carved up Europe to serve their own interests and ensure that monarchies would remain in place across the continent. They ignored the growing ethnic desires of Italy, Germany, Poland, and other peoples to become modern nations.

Note from the Future: The congress did not resolve the problems of Europe, but only postponed them. The seeds of World War I (exactly one hundred years in the future—1914) were laid at the Congress of Vienna in 1814–1815 (Mee 1993, 98–136).

- Quick Write: In a short paragraph, give an example in your life of a time when you did not finish a job you needed to do and it kicked back at you later for a second time. Then you had to do much more work this second time because you did not finish it the first time.
- Bumper Sticker: Create a bumper sticker for all the royal carriages at the Congress of Vienna urging them to recognize the new nations of Europe.
- Poster Power: Create a poster illustrating all the nobility of Europe gathered at the Congress of Vienna trying to turn the clock back to before the French Revolution.
- Share Pair: With a partner, take two major viewpoints of the Congress of Vienna—a royal view and an antiroyal, nationalist's view— and create a mock argument to present each of their points of view in front of the class.
- Front Page: In teams of four, as editors of the *Industrial Times* newspaper, create a front-page edition describing the Congress of Vienna. Be sure to include interviews with the royalists leading the congress and the nationalists who are being excluded from the deliberations.

- Map It: On a blank map of Europe, illustrate the major changes the Congress of Vienna made to the map of Europe and the future national problem areas that the congress ignored.
- ADV Futurist: Research your library for examples of problems that were left unresolved by the Congress of Vienna and that later became major wars or revolutions against the monarchs put in power at Vienna in 1815.

6.4.2   The Meiji Restoration (1868)

Never in the history of the world has a country changed so fast as Japan did during the Meiji Restoration between 1868 and 1912. At the start of 1868, Japan was still in the feudal age of Tokugawa shoguns (military governors) who ruled Japan alongside the traditional ancient emperor, acting as a figurehead. The Tokugawa lords still lived in their magnificent castles guarded by their samurai knights in armor and the peasants still toiled the land for their lords and masters. This picture of Japan at the start of the nineteenth century was right out of the Middle Ages in Europe—one thousand years before—the only problem was that this was the nineteenth century! This feudal existence ended in 1868 when both the shogun and the emperor died within a few months of each other. Japan was caught between its traditionalists and the modernists—a return to the old ways, or a chance to become modern. Influenced by contact with the American admiral Perry, Dutch merchants, and Jesuit missionaries, the modern leaders of Japan won out over the traditional leaders. In addition, the Japanese did not want to be dominated by the Westerners in the same manner that China was. The decision was made to modernize, but with some traditional trappings. The new emperor, Meiji (Enlightened Government)—only fifteen years old—was made the sole ruler of Japan without a shogun. A Japanese Parliament was created, but by the divine gift of the emperor, not by a human natural right of political representation. Promising students were immediately sent all over the world to study and learn Western ways and thinking. Western writers from Shakespeare to Marx were translated quickly into Japanese. Western ideas, clothes, and thinking were also imported as quickly as possible. By the end of the nineteenth century, "modern" Japan now had railways, telegraph wires, modern schools across the country, modern steel industries, baseball teams, and a modern, fully trained army and navy ready to fight the wars of the twentieth century. They even had a modern, nationalistic, Shinto spirit for fighting wars in the coming twentieth century (Ellwood 1980, 47–52).

- Quick Write: Think back to the last time you really changed your mind about something. You believed something very strongly, but then changed your mind to believe something else. How long did it take you to make the change? Write a short paragraph describing this personal change and share it with the class.
- Poster Power: Create a poster to be used in Japan during the Meiji Restoration to convince the Japanese to modernize.
- Bumper Sticker: Create a bumper sticker for use during the Meiji Restoration.
- Role Play: In teams of four, create short skits that illustrate how four different Japanese would have viewed the changes of the Meiji Restoration:
  1. Takuri Yamoto—a traditional samurai knight
  2. Jodoshin—a Shinto priest
  3. Haruki—a young hip Japanese teenager
  4. Yashimi—a Japanese schoolteacher
- ADV Historical Analysis: Look throughout history to find other examples of countries that have quickly changed and compare them to the Meiji Restoration in Japan.
- ADV The Futurist: Imagine the shock of Russia and the rest of the world when Japan defeated Russia in a war in 1905. All the odds were on Russia—a European country—winning the war against old-fashioned Japan, but the reverse happened. Research the Russo-Japanese War of 1905 in your library and then report to the class on your findings.

6.5.0 SOCIAL AND ECONOMIC LIFE

6.5.1 The Agricultural Revolution

Capitalism was invented in England during the agricultural revolution of the seventeenth and eighteenth centuries. Two words are the center of this revolution—"improvement" and "farmer." "Improvement" comes from the French *im* (into) and *pros* (profit). The word "farmer" means "tenant" who is renting the land to make "improvements"—to make the land profitable.

During the Middle Ages, nobles held the land and consumed what the peasants produced for them; the peasants survived on what was left. Each village also held common land upon which peasants were allowed to graze their sheep and cattle. This was the case for most of Europe as late as 1800, except for England.

Large landholders in England had begun to lease their land to "tenant" farmers in 1600 to grow grain and raise sheep to "improve" their land—to make a profit. The farmers hired workers to grow the grain and raise the sheep. This leasing of land by large landholders to farmers and the hiring of workers created the agricultural revolution. The farmers began to work hard to "improve" the land for their own profit, creating surplus grain and sheep to sell. The large landholders also began to "enclose" common village land and force peasants off the land in order to "improve" more land for profit. These landless peasants moved to large cities such as London and created a surplus labor class of workers. More people in the cities created larger markets for more grain and sheep. By 1800, England had a capitalist economy with large farms producing surplus food, a large urban workforce ready to work in the factories of the coming industrial revolution, and a need for more markets to sell their large surplus and turn it into profits (Palmer 1974, 101–107; Wood 1998, 14–31).

- Quick Write: In your own words, describe how you could make a profit out of something you know how to make.
- Poster Power: In teams of four, create a poster comparing the economic system of the Middle Ages with the new capitalistic, agricultural, economic system of England in 1800.
- Bumper Sticker: Create a bumper sticker for the landowners, the farmers, or the workers during the agricultural revolution in England.
- Diagram It: Create a circle of production to explain what was happening during the agricultural revolution, with farmers becoming richer with surplus food produced, more workers in the city buying the food, and the farmers producing even more.
- Editorial Staff: In teams of four, produce a special front-page edition of the *Industrial Times* that focuses on the agricultural revolution in England. Be sure to interview workers, farmers, and landowners on what is happening in England.
- Map It: On a blank map of the world, show how the idea of the agricultural revolution started in England and spread to Europe, the United States, and then to the rest of the world.

- ADV Acorns: Research how such a small new idea (an "acorn"), such as tenant farmers making a profit on the land in 1600, could explode into the dominant economic system of the world during the late twentieth century.

6.5.2   England's Industrial Revolution

The industrial revolution radically changed the face of England during the early nineteenth century. More people began to live in the cities than in the countryside. The population of England doubled during the first half of the century. Coal production doubled. Iron production quadrupled. Cotton imports quadrupled. The long Napoleonic Wars after 1799 also stimulated the industrial revolution in England by artificially creating the need for more guns, warships, uniforms, and food. Between 1806 and 1808, England produced three million gun barrels to meet the demand. The main industrial revolution in England, however, took place specifically in the textile industry. By the 1830s, England was importing more than 280 million tons of raw cotton each year from the American South and elsewhere, weaving it into cloth, and selling it around the world cheaper than anyone else could make it.

- Quick Write: Examine the shirt or blouse you are wearing. In a short paragraph, describe how you would cut and sew the shirt or blouse out of a single piece of cloth.
- Poster Power: Create a poster that illustrates the huge impact the industrial revolution had on England.
- Front Page: In teams of four editors (students), create a front-page edition of the *Industrial Times* newspaper discussing the impact of the industrial revolution on England. Be sure to illustrate your front page and interview major people affected by the industrial revolution.
- Music Mart: Create a song or a rap that celebrates the industrial revolution.
- ADV What If?: Create a scenario that describes what would happen if the industrial revolution had never taken place. What would lives be like today without it?

6.5.3   "General Lud's" Army (1811)

The Luddites went around England smashing the new machines and inventions of the industrial revolution between 1811 and 1813. They smashed new threshers in farmer's fields. They smashed power looms in the textile factories. The worst riots, however, were in the markets where the merchants refused to lower the price on potatoes—women outright attacked and captured wagons bringing potatoes to market. They said their leader was "General Lud" and that their actions were no joke. It took 12,000 soldiers to finally quell the Luddite Riots in 1813.

The many new inventions and machines of the industrial revolution made things easier, faster, and cheaper—for the capitalists who owned the factories but *not* for the workers who were being replaced by the machines. The Luddites realized this and destroyed thousands of the new industrial machines that were putting them out of work. The Luddite riots were much more complex than just being an anti-industrial revolution, however. In reality, there was no "General Lud"—he was just a worker who had smashed weaving machines some thirty years before. The riots were also not directly caused by the new inventions. It was wartime and England was at war with Napoleon. The bad weather between 1811 and 1813 caused exceptionally bad harvests across England and Europe. Napoleon's "Continental System" effectively cut off most English exports to the rest of Europe. The United States' Non-Importation Act, enforced in 1811, also cut another major source of exports for British factories. These factors resulted in skyrocketing food prices at a time when large numbers of workers were laid off due to the lack of markets for factory products. The new machines of the industrial revolution were more a symbol of frustration during a period of high food prices and laid-off workers (Gay 1966, 107–110; Palmer 1974, 38–45).

- Quick Write: In a short paragraph, give an example of a time when you and some friends were angry at something. Did you react just verbally or with violence?
- Graffiti: On a large piece of paper, create a wall graffiti the Luddites might use during the industrial revolution.
- Diary Entry #1: As a housewife of a recently laid-off factory worker, describe in your diary your anger of being unable to care for your family due to the hard times and the new machines.
- Diary Entry #2: As the inventor of a new machine for the industrial revolution, describe your anger at seeing your machine destroyed by the Luddites.
- Diary Entry #3: As an investor in the new machines of the industrial revolution, express your anger at the violence done against your investment, which is forcing you to lose money.

- Poster Power: Create a poster that illustrates the progress of the industrial revolution in making work and life easier, but also the frustrations of the Luddites who did not see its benefits.
- Song Fest: Create a theme song for the Luddites.
- Counter Song Fest: Create a theme song for the factory owners against the Luddites.
- Pros and Cons: In a team of four, create a short skit that illustrates both the positive and negative aspects of the Luddites.
- Front Page: In an editorial team (of four students) working for the *Industrial Times*—the leading newspaper of the nineteenth century—create a front-page, special edition on the Luddites. Be sure to include interviews with Luddite leaders, factory owners, and soldiers guarding the factories.
- ADV Historical Analysis: Research the Luddite movement in your library. Based on your reading, create a plan by which the violence of the Luddites could have been avoided.
- ADV The Futurist #1: The industrial revolution was the result of many new ideas and inventions that made life easier, but unfortunately put many people in old-fashioned jobs (such as those held by many Luddites) out of work. Using your library, make a list of the many inventions of the nineteenth century. With this list, create a list of new skills and jobs for which unemployed Luddites could train themselves.
- ADV The Futurist #2: Create a hypothetical story from the near future when computers take over and put almost everybody out of work. Will a neo-Luddite movement arise and start smashing computers, or will everybody be smart enough to learn new skills and create new jobs to keep themselves employed?

6.5.4 Capitalism or Socialism?

Who should benefit from the profits of the new factories of the industrial revolution—the capitalist owners or the workers? Two groups had very different ideas on this subject during the nineteenth century—Robert Owen (1771–1885) on one side and Thomas Malthus and David Ricardo on the other. Robert Owen was a factory owner who believed that the workers in his factories—if treated well with good pay, decent working hours, and safe working conditions—would work harder, produce more, and buy more, thereby making a higher profit for both the owner and the workers. Owen created a successful and profitable factory and community in New Lanark, Scotland, in 1805 based on his ideas of treating workers equally and fairly. Owen used the word "socialist" for the first time to describe his successful worker's factory and community. It became the model for "socialist" thinking in the future. Owen, however, never tried to expand his ideas to include governmental policy; he remained just a "socialist" in ideas rather than practice—a "utopian socialist."

Malthus and Ricardo believed in the "laissez-faire" (free market) economics of Adam Smith (see TLP 5.5.1), but for much more negative reasons. Smith believed that workers should be paid well so they could buy more in a free market system. Malthus disagreed. He believed the human population grew much faster than the food supply to feed them and that only disease, disaster, warfare, and famine kept the population in check. According to Malthus, if workers were paid high wages, received better working conditions, or received government assistance, they would produce more kids who would eat more food and create more famines. Ricardo called this the "Iron Law of Wages"—higher wages equals more children, more food consumed, and more workers competing for jobs. This, in turn, would depress wages, put people out of work, and create famine (see Palmer 1974, 116–117).

Note from the Future: The economic struggle between "socialist" beliefs in high wages for workers and negative "laissez-faire" beliefs in low wages for workers continues today across the world.

- Quick Write: Think for a moment about your future. If you receive a good-paying job, do you plan to have more children or do you plan on spending your money on a good car, a fine house, and a great music system? (Using your own future plans, which of the above economic systems are you modeling?)
- Venn Diagram: Create a Venn diagram that compares the differences and similarities between Owen and Malthus.
- Poster Power: Create a poster that illustrates the debate between Owen and Malthus concerning whether workers should be paid high or low wages.
- Time Traveler: Travel back in time to invite both Owen and Malthus (student actors in nineteenth-century dress) to join your class for a day. The students of your class can then prepare questions to ask both economic thinkers.
- ADV Historical Analysis: Using your library for resources, pick a country and then analyze its economic system to see whether it follows Owen or Malthus.

- ADV The Futurist: Using your library and the Internet as resources, examine the major economic policies of the major political parties today. Do you think they follow the policies of either Owen or Malthus?

6.5.5 Workers of the World Unite (1848)

Karl Marx (1818–1883) and Friedrich Engles (1825–1895) were socialists who listened to Robert Owen, but they were not satisfied with "utopian socialism." They wanted to implement a more revolutionary workers (proletariat) movement that would overthrow the existing rulers and factory owners (bourgeoisie) in order to form a country run by the workers. All history, said Marx and Engles in their *Communist Manifesto* (1848), was a class struggle between the property owners and those without property. In prehistory, there was no personal property; everything was shared in a "communist" society. During the Middle Ages, the kings and nobles held the property and the peasants did not. During the Renaissance and Enlightenment, the growing merchant class became the class with property (the bourgeoisie) and imposed their will on those without property (the proletariat). During the nineteenth century, the leaders of the industrial revolution (the capitalist factory owners) became the bourgeoisie who imposed their will on the proletariat workers. Eventually, said Marx and Engles, the growing masses of the proletariat would realize their power, rise up to overthrow the bourgeoisie, and create a state run by the proletariat. This eventually would be replaced by a pure communist state in which all property would again be shared.

Note from the Future: Marx and Engles were not able to implement their plan for a workers' state during their lifetimes. A revolutionary by the name of Lenin, however, took the ideas of Marx and Engles and created a "communist" state out of Russia in 1917 (Palmer 1974, 118–126).

- Quick Write: Should everyone share all property or should individuals be allowed to own their own property? Write a short paragraph on the reasons for your decision.
- Slogan: Marx and Engles are tired of their slogan "Workers of the World Unite!" Create a new catchy slogan they can use for their communist movement.
- Venn Diagram: Using a Venn diagram, compare the similarities and differences between the utopian socialism of Robert Owen and the communist thinking of Marx and Engles.

- You Were There: As the host of this popular TV program during the nineteenth century, your upcoming guests will be Marx and Engles (students in costume). The studio audience (students in class) should each prepare at least three questions to ask our distinguished guests this week.
- Poster Power: Create a poster that illustrates the major ideas of Marx and Engles.
- Perspectives: In a team of four (students), create a small skit that illustrates four different points of view concerning the thinking of Marx and Engles:
  1. Jethro Brick—a factory worker who has recently lost his job
  2. F. T. Porker—a factory owner concerned about the profits earned by his company
  3. Maria Shelly—the owner of a small store who likes to pay her workers a fair wage
  4. Bart Thunker—the local policeman who hates violence
- ADV Historical Analysis: Compare the early Christian communities described in the Bible with the communist communities described by Marx and Engles during the nineteenth century.
- ADV The Futurist: Analyze why the Soviet Union and China during the late twentieth century abandoned the teaching of Marx and Engles in favor of the laissez-faire teachings of Adam Smith.

6.6.0   RELIGIOUS THOUGHT

6.6.1   Missionary Movement—The White Man's Burden

A Christian evangelical revival movement swept Europe during the late eighteenth and early nineteenth centuries. A major call of this revival movement was to go out and preach the word of God to everyone on Earth. The Jesuit and Franciscan orders of the Catholic Church had been doing missionary work since the time of the Reformation across most regions of the world. This new Christian revival movement of the late eighteenth and early nineteenth centuries, however, was restricted, for the most part, to the Protestant churches. Africa became a central focal point for these new missionaries, in part due to the abolitionist movement against African slavery taking place in England at the same time. The early nineteenth century was also the era of the industrial revolution, with Europe producing a large surplus of manufactured goods to sell to new markets across the globe. These new markets for European manufactured goods became the centers for Christian missionaries. The missionaries, in turn, became the explorers and unofficial agents of the European governments. The Christian missionaries "civilized" (Europeanized) their converts to think, act, and dress like Europeans. Many missionaries really did not intend to have the governments of Europe follow them and establish colonies, but when they got in trouble, they quickly called on European governments to assist them. Without really planning to have formal colonies, the governments of Europe found themselves defending and ruling many regions of Africa and the world.

David Livingstone (1813–1873) was an interesting example of such an English missionary. He worked for many years among the Bakwena people of Botswana as a missionary, a trader, and even a military instructor. Due to his influence, the Bakwena were able to defend themselves with modern weapons against attacks from the Dutch European settlers in South Africa. Although he was called a missionary, Livingstone was best known for his explorations in southern, central, and eastern Africa. More European and American traders and missionaries quickly followed Livingstone's footsteps. Livingstone, however, was highly critical of so many European and American missionaries in Africa, preferring instead that Africans be appointed as Christian missionaries to their own people. He sensed that the large number of European and American missionaries entering Africa was leading to European control of Africa and he opposed it. Livingstone was right. Within twenty years, these same areas became parts of the colonial empires of England, France, Germany, and Belgium (see also TLP 6.3.5 European Imperialism).

- Quick Write: Imagine a foreigner with strange clothes and speaking a strange language coming into your neighborhood and working to convert you to his religion. Write a short paragraph about how you would react.
- Map It: On a blank map of Africa, trace the route of Livingstone's explorations from Botswana through Zimbabwe, Zambia, Malawi, Tanzania, and Kenya.
- Front Page: In an editorial team of four students, create a front-page edition of the *Industrial Times* newspaper that focuses on the missionary movement of the nineteenth century. Be sure to interview— from students in your class—at least one missionary, one recent convert, and one strongly opposed to the missionaries.

- Bumper Sticker #1: Create a bumper sticker for a missionary wagon heading into Africa during the nineteenth century.
- Bumper Sticker #2: Create a bumper sticker for someone in Africa opposed to foreign missionaries coming into his or her country.
- Poster Power: Create a poster that illustrates how the missionary movement fit into the general imperial expansion of Europe during the nineteenth century.
- ADV Historical Analysis: Research your library for information on the long-range impact of three aspects of the missionary movement in Africa:
  1. Was the movement successful during the past 200 years in converting large numbers of Africans to Christianity?
  2. Would the movement have been more successful if it had followed Livingstone's advice 150 years ago and used African rather than European and American missionaries?
  3. What image did the missionaries create of Africa for the Europeans and Americans back home? How did this image affect current American and European relations with countries in Africa?

6.7.0   CONQUEST AND WARFARE

6.7.1   Britannia Rules the Waves

The Battle of Trafalgar (1805) was one of the high points in British history. Lord Nelson's fleet of gigantic square-riggers caught the French fleet off the coast of Spain and destroyed eighteen of thirty-three French ships. The battle ended any threat of a French invasion of England by Napoleon and it insured England's domination of the oceans for the rest of the nineteenth century. The superiority of British sea power also enabled England to create its overseas empire of colonies "on which the sun never set."

The massive three-deck, sailing batteries of England and France — firing 100 cannons each — were a fearsome sight at Trafalgar, with clouds of smoke, burning ships, and thousands of dying men. Far worse, however, were the living conditions for the common sailors. Sailors were paid two shillings sixpence (twenty-six cents) a week to live in cramped, damp quarters on salt beef and maggoty biscuits with the threat of fifty lashes for disobedience. Twelve times more sailors died from disease than battle in the nineteenth-century British navy.

Ten thousand more sailors deserted the British navy during the Napoleonic Wars than were killed in battle. The only way England could keep its ships full of men was to raid small towns and other ships in order to capture—impress—men to work on its ships. Such impressment of sailors by England from the American ships led to a small conflict called "The War of 1812" (Palmer 1974, 46–55).

- Quick Write: Imagine what it was like to be in a nineteenth-century naval battle—the smoke, the roaring cannons, the crashing sails, the dying men. In a short paragraph, give a description of the way it might have been if you were there.
- Stern Sticker: Create a stern sticker for the backside of one of the French or British ships in the Battle of Trafalgar.
- Painter's Corner: Find some pictures of nineteenth-century ships in your library, and from these create a dramatic painting of the gigantic ships fighting each other during the Battle of Trafalgar. When finished, share your masterpiece with the class.
- Quick Skit: In teams of four, develop a short skit that illustrates the life of British sailors during the nineteenth century.
- Poster Power: Create a poster that illustrates how the Battle of Trafalgar was one of history's turning points.
- Reader's Corner: Read one of the Horatio Hornblower books about life in the British navy during the nineteenth century and report back to your class on your reading.
- Front Page: As the team of the four major editors of the *Industrial Times* newspaper—the leading news rag of the nineteenth century— create a front-page edition of the paper on the Battle of Trafalgar and include an exposé on the treatment of sailors in the British navy.
- ADV Historical Analysis: After reading more about the effects of the Battle of Trafalgar in your library, compare the effects of this battle to other major turning points in history. Report your findings to the class.

6.7.2   Lieutenant Napoleon Bonaparte

A little-known French lieutenant named Bonaparte ended the French Revolution in 1799 and took control of France. In 1804, he crowned himself "emperor" with the approval of the French people and the pope in Rome. The new emperor had grand designs for a unified European empire. Immediately, his armies began to conquer most of Europe. By 1807, some twenty nations of Europe were part of Napoleon's grand European empire, including Austria, Prussia, Italy, and Spain—but not England. Many, if not most, of the common people of Europe welcomed him as a liberator. Everywhere he conquered, he abolished the feudal system of the nobility. Under his rule, Europe received a unified European army, a unified law code and court system that promoted equal and civil liberties, and a unified system of highways—including driving on the right-hand side of the road. Napoleon had even bigger ideas: with 700,000 soldiers from most of Europe and careful planning, he attacked Russia in late June of 1812. He thought it was going to be an easy conquest. With heavy losses, Napoleon captured a deserted Moscow in September of 1812. His army was exhausted and low on supplies. With winter coming on, he began to retreat across a barren Russian landscape with temperatures reaching thirty below zero. Three-quarters of Napoleon's army was lost in Russia—400,000 in death and 100,000 as prisoners of war. With his Russian defeat, Napoleon's empire quickly collapsed. The gleeful former kings and nobles of Europe gathered at the Congress of Vienna in 1814–1815 to party and to divide up Europe (see also TLP 6.4.1 The Congress of Vienna; Palmer 1974, 26–27, 46–55).

- Quick Write: Which is better—a unified continent under one dictator who treats everyone fairly, or many small governments ruled by kings and nobles, with no rights for the common people? In a short paragraph, describe the reasons for your decisions.
- Rumper Sticker: Create a rumper sticker for Napoleon's horse, indicating either your support or opposition to Napoleon.
- Picture Bias: Create two drawings of what you think Napoleon Bonaparte might have looked like. One drawing should show him as a hero ending the power of the nobility in Europe. The other drawing should show him as a villain who is destroying the good old days when the kings and nobles ruled Europe.
- Poster Power: Create a poster that compares Napoleon as both a hero and a villain of the French Revolution.
- Quick Skit #1: In a team of four, develop and present to the class a skit that illustrates the suffering and thoughts of Napoleon's soldiers as they retreated from Moscow in 1812 and the joy of the Russians who watched them leave.
- Quick Skit #2: In a team of four, develop and present a skit to the class that illustrates the utter joy the former kings and queens of Eu-

rope felt when they heard that Napoleon was defeated by Russia's winter in 1812.

- ADV Historical Analysis #1: Research your library to compare Napoleon with other leaders in history who overestimated their own powers and abilities. When finished, present your findings to the class.
- ADV Historical Analysis #2: Research your library and the Internet to compare dictatorships with democracies. Are all dictatorships bad and all democracies good, or have there been good dictatorships and bad democracies in history?
- ADV The Futurist: Research your library to compare Napoleon's conquest of Europe and Russia with Hitler's conquests during World War II.

6.7.3 Shaka Zulu

Shaka (1773–1828)—one of the major military geniuses in the history of the world—arose in the early nineteenth century in the Natal region of southern Africa. At a time in the world when the British were beginning to exert their imperial sea power around the world, the British were strongly threatened in southern Africa by this leader of a small clan called the Zulu. In 1816, Shaka built a giant war machine and national empire, which devastated most of southern and eastern Africa for several thousand miles. African warfare before Shaka was relatively informal—two sides throwing spears at each other. Shaka radically changed all this with short stabbing spears, large shields, and tightly organized regiments of highly trained soldiers. A Zulu army would attack an opposing army with a single regiment, falsify a retreat to draw the enemy forward, and strike quickly with two regiments attacking from both sides. This Zulu battle tactic of Shaka's was revolutionary and enabled the Zulu to capture large parts of southern Africa very quickly. Captured young men and women from each battle were not enslaved but rather quickly absorbed into a rapidly growing Zulu nation. Any African peoples not incorporated into the Zulu empire fled in terror. This fleeing of thousands of people from the Zulu was called the *Difaqane*. These *Difaqane* refugees fleeing from Shaka frightened the small British colony at Cape Town, South Africa. Other *Difaqane* refugees attacked the peoples of Botswana, Lesotho, Swaziland, Mozambique, Zimbabwe, Zambia, Malawi, and Tanzania, causing waves of warfare and bloodshed wherever they fled. In the end, Shaka self-destructed. His mother held a strange power over him; when she died, he went crazy killing his own people. His brother finally murdered him—to the relief of much of southern Africa.

Note from the Future: The Zulu are still one of the major peoples of South Africa today and are renowned for their prowess in warfare (Stuart and Malcolm 1950; Hamilton 1995).

- Quick Write: In a short paragraph, describe what you think a person would have to do to rise from being a common person to becoming one of the most famous leaders in history.
- Map Attack: On a blank map of Africa, locate the eastern state of Natal in South Africa and identify it as the home of the Zulu. With arrows and shading, then identify all the countries of southern and eastern Africa that were devastated by the *Difaqane* started by the Zulu.
- You Were There: As hosts of this top TV program during the nineteenth century, have the reporters in the audience (classroom) interview, with three questions each, some of the actual people who knew Shaka:
  1. Francis Fynn—one of the few Europeans to have visited Shaka and lived to tell about him
  2. Ngomane—one of Shaka's major generals
  3. Naledi—a Motswana princess who had to flee from the attacking armies of Shaka
  4. Mzilikazi—an African leader who fled from Shaka and founded an empire in Zimbabwe to the north
- Art Mart: Create a painting of a Zulu soldier of the early nineteenth century.
- Poster Power: Illustrate on a poster the power of Shaka's military tactics.
- ADV Historical Research: Using sources found in your library and on the Internet, trace the factors that enabled Shaka to rise to power and those factors that led to his early death.
- ADV What If?: How could Shaka have created his large empire by peaceful means? With a set of four partners, create such a plan and present it to your class.

6.7.4   Liberation, Not Revolution—Simón Bolívar

The aristocracy of Spain had lived in luxury for three centuries due to the steady supply of silver acquired from its empire in South America. This empire of the Americas ended when Simón Bolívar defeated a Peruvian Spanish army in 1824. The struggle for the liberation of South

America, however, was long and difficult. Bolívar started his conquest to liberate South America from Spanish rule when Napoleon invaded Spain in 1808. Bolívar's ultimate dream was for a united and independent South American republic. Bolívar's first attempt at conquest started in Venezuela, but it was a revolt mostly of rich, educated Creoles (Spanish people born in South America) against Spain and it was not successful. With his small, ill-equipped army, he retreated up into the high Andes Mountains of South America. He repeated this same action every time he was defeated but he did not give up his dream. With repeated failures of his Creole army against the Spanish, he began to recruit local Indians and former African slaves into his army and even a regiment of former English soldiers to fight for him. Always with small armies and very few supplies, Bolívar gained the respect of anti-Spanish leaders throughout South America. As a rich Creole, however, Bolívar was careful never to antagonize the rich landowners and Creole aristocracy wherever his armies traveled. He obtained local Indian and African support, who hoped that he would eventually lead a full revolution against the rich landowners as well as the Spanish, but Bolívar never abandoned his rich Creole roots. He was successful in raising local armies in Venezuela, Columbia, Ecuador, and Peru—but never for a liberating army for South America and never for a full revolution. He was successful in 1824 in defeating the last Spanish army in South America, but his supporters had no interest in his bigger dream of a South American republic. They wanted small local countries and quickly deserted Bolívar to found their own separate countries— Venezuela, Ecuador, Columbia, and Peru. Indian and African supporters of Bolívar also found that their leader had no interest in supporting their revolutionary cause against the rich Creole landowners of South America. Bolívar died alone in 1830 with his dream incomplete and very few supporters (Palmer 1974, 67–71).

Note from the Future: Today, the rich Creole landowners still control most of South America while the Indian and African populations still form the working and peasant class of the continent.

- Quick Write: Think for a moment about what it would take for you to support the liberation of a country from a foreign ruler. When ready, write a short paragraph about your support of a liberation movement and share it with the class.
- Rumper Sticker: Create a rumper sticker for Bolívar's horse, either for or against Bolívar's cause.

- Poster Power: Create a poster illustrating the strengths and weaknesses of Bolívar's struggle.
- Song Fest: Create a song or a rap about Bolívar.
- Madison Avenue: As the recently hired advertising firm to strengthen Bolívar's public relations image in South America, create an ad campaign for Bolívar with an ad slogan, a radio jingle, and a thirty-second TV spot.
- Front Page: As the editorial team (four students) of the leading newspaper of the nineteenth century, the *Industrial Times*, do a special front-page edition on Bolívar and his successes and failures. Be sure to include an illustration of Bolívar and interviews with people who supported and opposed him.
- ADV What If?: After researching Bolívar in the library, develop a plan by which Bolívar might have reached his full dream of a united South American republic.
- ADV The Futurist: The rich landowners versus the poor Indians is still the major problem in South America. Create a plan to resolve this problem.

6.8.0   TRAGEDY AND DISASTER

6.8.1   The Dark Side of the Industrial Revolution

The industrial revolution created working conditions the world had never seen before. People could no longer work at their own pace; instead, they had to keep up with the pace of machines that did not rest. Never in history had so much coal been burned, iron smelted, and cloth manufactured. The immense pollution problems that resulted were totally unexpected. The world had also never seen so many people packed into cities, so much crime, and so much raw sewage flowing in the streets. A Prussian traveler in 1814 graphically described the ecological conditions of the factory of Manchester in England during the industrial revolution: "The cloud of coal vapor may be observed from afar. The houses are blackened by it. The river which flows through Manchester is so filled with waste dye stuffs that it resembles a dyer's vat" (Palmer 1974).

The early industrial revolution had no air filters. Coal smoke filled the air and lungs of all who were nearby. It had no underground sewers; all sewage flowed down ditches in the streets. Clean drinking water was almost unheard of; at best, contaminated wells were the source of drinking water for most people.

After hearing many reports on the squalid conditions of children working in factories, the English Parliament passed the First Factory Act in 1802, over the strong objections of the factory owners who stated that such laws interfered with their profits. The major conditions of the First Factory Act were as follows (Palmer 1974, 36–37):

1. Factories are to be cleaned twice a year.
2. All workers are to receive one suit of working clothes per year.
3. Children can work no more than twelve hours per day.
4. Children are to receive one hour of religious instruction every Sunday.
5. A medical doctor should visit a factory if an epidemic breaks out.
6. Any factory that does not comply with these laws is to be fined five pounds (ten dollars).

- Quick Write: Describe the worst working and living conditions you have ever seen in a short paragraph.
- Graffiti: On a large piece of paper, create graffiti to protest the inhuman conditions of the industrial revolution. When finished, put it along the wall of your classroom.
- Protest Letter: Write a letter to your local parliamentarian (member of Congress) protesting the working and living conditions of the industrial revolution.
- Counter Spin: As a factory owner during the industrial revolution, write a letter to your parliamentarian describing the "excellent" working conditions in your factory, and be sure to mention the enclosed contribution made to his upcoming election campaign fund.
- Protest Song: Create a protest song focused on the working and living conditions of the poor workers during the industrial revolution.
- Poster Power: Make a poster illustrating the poor conditions for workers during the industrial revolution.
- Her Majesty's Workers Committee: As members of Her Majesty's Workers Committee (four students in each committee), make recommendations to be delivered to Parliament (your class) for the revision of the First Factory Act of 1802 for the betterment of the workers.
- Her Majesty's Factory Owners Committee: As members of Her Majesty's Factory Owners Committee (four students in each committee), make recommendations to be delivered to Parliament (your

class) for the revision of the First Factory Act of 1802 for the better-ment of the factory owners.

- ADV The Futurist #1: Research your library for what was done by the British government to improve the conditions for the workers during the nineteenth century.
- ADV The Futurist #2: Research your library to find out which prob-lems of the industrial revolution remained unsolved and lasted down through the twentieth century.

6.9.0   EXPLORATION AND DISCOVERY

6.9.1   The Nineteenth-Century Discovery of Electricity

Perhaps the greatest discovery of the nineteenth century was practical and portable electricity. Yes, we have all heard of Ben Franklin's dis-covery of electricity in lightning, but what did he do with his discov-ery? Nothing. Many eighteenth-century scholars also knew how to make electricity by friction for parlor tricks, but it was not very useful when you could not move it. Even the ancient Greeks knew how to make static electricity by friction ("elektron" is an ancient Greek word). Useful electricity was created through a series of interesting dis-coveries during the nineteenth century:

1. In 1800, the Italian physicist, Alessandro Volta (yes, volts are named after him), discovered that plates of zinc and silver lami-nated together produced chemical electricity as well as a battery, which could store electricity for a short time.
2. In 1820, the Danish physicist, Hans Christian Oersted, used Volta's electric battery and discovered that it moved a compass needle. He had discovered that electricity was magnetic.
3. The German, Georg Ohm (Ohm's Law), in 1826, discovered that different metals (such as copper and lead) resisted the flow of electrical current at different levels. He measured this electrical resistance with units he called "Volts."
4. In 1836, an American, Samuel Morse, using an electrical battery and a copper wire, sent the first electrical message by wire (using, of course, Morse code).
5. An Englishman, James Maxwell, mathematically unified friction, current, and chemical electricity together into a single unified the-

ory of electricity in 1864. With his new theory of unified electricity, he predicted the existence of electromagnetic waves that traveled the speed of light, as well as a different kind of sound wave he called "radio" waves.

6. In 1865, another American, Thomas Alva Edison, tied the theory and the practical aspects of electricity together with three inventions: first, an electromagnetic generator run by a steam engine; second, an electrical incandescent lamp (a light bulb); and third, an electrical metering system for billing customers.

By the end of the century, Edison's electrical light bulbs were lighting homes, factories, offices, and streets around the world — and the rest is history (Burchell 1966, 32–35).

- Quick Write: Describe in a short paragraph what life would be like without electricity. What things from life today would you miss the most if there were no electricity?
- Bumper Sticker: Create a bumper sticker for a nineteenth-century horse-drawn carriage that advertises one of Edison's new light bulbs.
- Poster Power: Create a poster that illustrates what the discovery of electricity did to the world.
- Time Line: In a team of four students, create a time line on a large piece of paper illustrating the amazingly quick series of discoveries and inventions during the early nineteenth century that led to the practical, everyday use of electricity across the world.
- You Were There: As the host of this popular TV program of the nineteenth century, have the members of your studio audience (students in class) prepare three questions each for our famous guests (students in costume) from the nineteenth century who are responsible for the electricity we use today: Volta, Oersted, Olm, Morse, Maxwell, and Edison.
- Quick Skit: In teams of four, create a short skit that illustrates the importance of one discovery following another to establish the initial preconditions for more discoveries and inventions to take place.
- ADV Historical Analysis: Think for a moment and identify what you think are the five most important discoveries in the history of humankind. How does the discovery and invention of the practical use of electricity rank in your list? Be prepared to present your list and defend your reasons in front of your class.

6.9.2   Darwin's *Origin of the Species*

In 1859, a very shy scientist by the name of Charles Darwin published his book, *Origin of the Species,* after many years of thoughtful reflection and study. Darwin did not want his book to cause any controversy. The book, however, created a controversy as large as those of Copernicus and Galileo several hundred years earlier when they simply noted that the Earth was not the center of the universe. All Darwin did was announce, after careful study, the four major points of his theory of evolution:

1. Plants and animals do not reproduce identical replicas of their kind.
2. Organisms, however, do reproduce variations of their kind, often with hereditary traits.
3. Nature allows only those species that are most fit to survive.
4. Out of this a struggle for survival comes a process called "the survival of the fittest."

As with Copernicus and Galileo before him, righteous Christian leaders in Europe and the United States raised the alarm that Darwin's theory of evolution was a direct challenge to the Book of Genesis in the Bible, which stated that God created the world in seven days. What Darwin stated, however, was not new. Eighteenth-century naturalists had already classified humans as a type of animal. Geologists and thinkers as far back as da Vinci knew that the fossil record of seashells and bones imbedded in rock thousands of feet above the ocean were clear indications that the Earth was not created in seven days. What Darwin did, however, was simply and clearly state the current consensus of scientific thinking about evolution during the middle of the nineteenth century. Darwin's theory of evolution also introduced the idea of "progress" to human thinking. Evolution was not a set process determined ahead of time. Humans, through their own choices and hard work, can create "progress" and determine the direction of the future (Burchell 1966, 37–38).

- Quick Write: In a short paragraph, describe a fossil you have seen and how old you think it might be.
- Bumper Sticker: Create a bumper sticker either promoting Darwin or opposing him when his book was first published in 1859.

- Poster Power: Create a poster that illustrates the controversy between the scientific thinking of Darwin and the righteous Christian leaders of his day.
- Music Mart: With a partner, compose a short song or rap that tells the story of Darwin and the trouble he had with many Christian leaders of the nineteenth century.
- Front Page: With a team of four student editors, create a front-page edition of the *Industrial Times* newspaper that focuses on the controversy between Darwin and the Christian leaders of the nineteenth century. Be sure to interview representative from both views of the controversy and have an editorial column in which you state your own views.
- ADV Historical Comparison: Which was a greater scientific controversy with the Christian church: Copernicus's and Galileo's discoveries, or Darwin's discoveries? Research both controversies in your library and present your findings to the class.
- ADV What If?: What if Darwin never developed the concept of "progress"—that humans can make themselves better? What would be the future of humans without this idea?
- ADV The Futurist: In your community today, interview a scientist or science teacher concerning the importance of Darwin's theory of evolution and a "creationist" who does not believe that humans and animals evolve.

6.10.0 INVENTION AND REVOLUTION

6.10.1 Fulton's Folly

Contrary to what many people believe, Robert Fulton (1765–1815) did not invent the first steamboat. He was an American painter, he built canals in England, and he built a submarine for Napoleon in France, but the first known steamboat was built in France in 1773. It sank. James Ramsey in Maryland built and tested a jet-powered steamboat in 1787, but he died before he could finish it. John Fitch of Connecticut built a steamboat with power oars, but drank himself to death. Other steamships were built in England, but ran out of financial backing. In 1803, Robert Fulton was in France working on submarines. By accident, he met Robert Livingston, the American ambassador to France, and the two talked about steamboats. Livingston was rich and held the monopoly to run steamboats on the Hudson River in New York, but he did not have a steamboat. Fulton and Livingston created a partnership to build steamboats to run on the Hudson. Several problems stood in the way. The only steam engine factory in the world was in England, and England was at war with France. No problem. Fulton traveled to England under the assumed name of "Francis" to hide the fact that he had previously built submarines for the French. After a delay of several years, Fulton was granted a permit to export an English steam engine to the United States to build a steamboat. Fulton also assured Livingston's financial support by marrying Livingston's daughter. In 1807, Fulton built a small practical paddlewheel steamboat and ran it upriver from New York City to Albany in thirty-two hours. People along the river at first thought it was a sea monster or the end of the world when they saw its shower of sparks and heard its clanging noises at night. Others called it "Fulton's Folly." The forty people who first made the trip, however, thought it was great. By 1809, many improvements later, "Fulton's Folly" became a financial success—the first commercially successful steamboat in the world and one of the major inventions of the industrial revolution (Palmer 1974, 28–35).

- Quick Write: Sit back for a moment and think of an invention that would greatly improve how we live. Write a quick paragraph about this invention and share your ideas with the class.
- Chart It: In a team of four, create a large chart illustrating the history of all the failed steamboats prior to Fulton's successful model and present it to your class. Analyze your chart and add at least three conclusions that we can draw from it. Your conclusions should focus on what your chart tells us about inventing things and making them successful in the future.
- Stern Sticker: Create a stern sticker for Fulton's first steamboat on the Hudson River.
- List It: Make a list of all the factors that Fulton had to overcome before he could make the first commercially successful steamboat.
- Concept Web: Inventions almost always help people to do things better. Using the word "steamboat" as the central concept on the board, have the class list all of the things they can imagine a "steamboat" could do that would make life easier for everybody else.
- Poster Power: Create a poster that advertises the new Fulton steamboat.
- Model It: Create a cardboard model of Fulton's first steamboat.
- Counter Spin: With a partner, make a list of negative contributions of the steamboat (for example, pollution).

- Perspectives: In teams of four, role-play four different perspectives concerning Fulton's steamboat:
  1. T. T. Tuttle—a proud investor in Fulton's steamboat
  2. Malcolm Merkin—the owner of a fruit shop who now could sell fresh fruit in the next town upriver
  3. P. T. Stump—an angry sailboat captain who lost his transport business to the steamboat
  4. Gerty Murtle—a homeowner on the river who complained about all the noise and coal smoke from the new steamboat
- ADV The Futurist: Based on research in your library or on the Internet, make a time line from 1807 to the present on the different types of power boats that have been used since the steamboat replaced the sailboat.

6.10.2   Inventions, Inventions, Inventions

The industrial revolution was an explosion of inventions such as the following (Gay 1966, 102–107):
  1. Jethro Tull, an Englishman, the seed-planting machine (1701)
  2. Robert Fulton, an American, the first steamboat (1807)
  3. Henry Bessemer, an Englishman, the first blast furnace to make steel (1850)
  4. Edward Cartwright, an Englishman, the water-powered loom for weaving (1785)
  5. Eli Whitney, an American, the cotton gin and the idea of interchangeable parts for manufacturing (1793)
  6. Joseph Bramah, an Englishman, the modern water closet (1778)
  7. Henry Cort, an Englishman, rolled iron (1784)
  8. Joseph Jacquard, a Frenchman, a silk power loom (1800)
  9. Thomas Newcomen, an Englishman, the steam pump (1712)
  10. Samuel Morse, an American, the telegraph (1837)
  11. James Watt, an Englishman, the steam engine (1769)
  12. Richard Trivithick, an Englishman, the first train driven by a steam engine (1804)
  13. James Sharp, an Englishman, the winnowing machine (1777)
  14. James Hargrave, an Englishman, the spinning jenny (1768)
  15. Michael Menzies, an Englishman, the threshing machine (1732)
- Quick Write: Think of a major invention you would like to see made. Write a short paragraph describing it and then present this idea to the class.

- Chart It: Create a chart that illustrates the number of major inventions created by the Americans, the English, and the French.
- 3D Map Attack: Attach the name and a drawing of each of the above inventions (if possible) to a 6"-x-4" card and tape each to a display table. When completed, attach a map of the world to a standing piece of cardboard or Styrofoam behind the table. Now attach a piece of colored twine or string to each invention and connect each piece of string to the country of origin on the map. What conclusions can now be drawn from this dynamic display of nineteenth-century inventions?
- You Were There: As the host of this popular TV program during the industrial revolution, fourteen of the major inventors (students) of the agricultural and industrial revolutions will briefly describe and demonstrate their inventions. The studio audience (students in the class) before the show can prepare three questions each for these inventors who will be your guests for the evening.
- Time Line: As a class project, place all the inventions in chronological order, create illustrations for each invention, and then make a large time line across one wall of your classroom of the major inventions of the era.
- ADV Diorama: Create a diorama or model of one of the major inventions of the agricultural or industrial revolutions.

6.11.0 ART AND CREATIVE THOUGHT

6.11.1 The Fury of the Sea at Dusk—The Birth of Impressionism

No artist better represents the change from the eighteenth century to the nineteenth century than the English painter J. M. W. Turner (1775–1851). His early paintings during the turn of the century reflect the realistic romantic landscapes of Europe during the Enlightenment. Slowly and cautiously during the early nineteenth century, Turner started to paint the fury of the sea, swirling clouds in storms, and the intensity of the setting sun on ships and sails. As the nineteenth century progressed, Turner's paintings became less the realistic romantic paintings and more the impressions of light, wind, weather, and sea on a ship or a building. Turner's paintings also reflected the new nineteenth-century scientific understanding of light as the separate continuum of color expressed by the rainbow. Suddenly, bright colors were everywhere in swirls of light in Turner's paintings. Many old painters grumbled about Turner—too colorful and too fuzzy they said; good paintings should be dark and dreary. A young French painter named Claude Monet disagreed. Monet chanced upon Turner's paintings in London and immediately began to use Turner's techniques of light and color in his paintings. Other French painters, such as Manet, Degas, Renoir, and Van Gogh, also began to follow the same style—they called it *impressionism*. The old classical painters still grumbled about the fuzzy paintings with too much color, and the impressionists initially did not become popular in Europe. It was only when American, Russian, and Japanese painters began to buy large numbers of impressionist paintings that European buyers began to take a second look at impressionism and purchase them in large numbers (Wilton 1979).

Note from the Future: Today, we recognize impressionism as the major symbolic art form of the nineteenth century. The paintings of the nineteenth-century impressionists are now purchased for millions of dollars by collectors around the world.

- Quick Write: In a short paragraph, describe the fury of the ocean in a storm at sunset. When finished, share your impressions of this event with the class.
- Sketch Pad: Make two sketches of the same person or thing: one an eighteenth-century realistic depiction of the person or thing, and the other a nineteenth-century impressionist image of the person or thing. Share your sketches with the class.
- Bumper Sticker: Create a nineteenth-century bumper sticker either for or against impressionism to be placed on the back of the horse-drawn carriages of the period.
- Poet's Corner: Write a short poem describing the image of a favorite impressionist painting of yours and share it with the class.
- Role Play: With a partner, role-play a stuffy old classical painter wanting clear, realistic paintings with dark colors and a new impressionist painter wanting the personal feeling of color and light to dominate paintings.
- ADV Action T Chart: Using your library or Internet as resources, look at a realistic painting from the eighteenth century and a nineteenth-century impressionist painting. Describe the differences you see.
- ADV Historical analysis: The nineteenth century is mostly known for its grimy, gray factories and inhuman working conditions. Nineteenth-century impressionist painting, however, is renowned for its bright colors, swirls of light, and peaceful country scenes. Research

your library and the Internet to discover why there is such a contrast between the dirty, gray, nineteenth-century factories of Europe and the bright, cheery paintings of the impressionists of the same time.

6.11.2   Taoist Impressionism—The Painted Word

"To paint the bamboo," said the Chinese artist and scholar Su Shih, "one must have it entirely within one. Grasp the brush, look intently [at the paper], then visualize what you are going to paint. Follow your vision quickly, lift your brush and pursue directly that which you see [in your mind], as a falcon dives on the springing hare—the least slackening and it will escape you" (Boorstin 1992).

The pen, writing the word of God, was holy according to the Christian iconoclasts and the Muslims during the early Middle Ages. Brushes that painted images, however, were the work of the devil. As a result, artistic painting in Europe almost did not come into existence. It never took place in the Muslim Middle East.

Although the pen/written word and the brush/painted image were forever separated in the West, they were as one in Taoist China and Japan. Writing in Chinese and Japanese was always done with a brush, never a pen. As a result, calligraphy—the art of writing—was just as important as the words of a poem. The distinction between scholars and artists from Europe did not exist in China. Western painting focused on human or religious portraits, and landscape painting did not appear until the nineteenth century in Europe. The opposite is true of Eastern painting. Landscape painting was always the center of Chinese and Japanese painting, with the human subject always small and insignificant. The chi'i—the way of nature—was supreme to the individual human in China. The European impressionist painter Monet would paint quickly by a bridge to see the light reflecting on the bridge in just the right way. The Chinese Taoist painter would stare intently at a blank paper in front of him until he saw the image he wanted to paint. He would then paint quickly before the image left him (Boorstin 1992, 419–426).

- Quick Draw: Close your eyes until you can imagine a leaf fallen from a tree. On a piece of paper, quickly draw the image of the leaf you saw in your mind.
- T Chart: Using a T chart, compare Western art and calligraphy with Chinese art and calligraphy.

Illustration 6.11.2 *Taoist Impressionist Poem Translated into Japanese [top to bottom]: Toten goshiki [no] kumo. Translated into English [top to bottom]: East, Heaven, Five, Color, Cloud.*

- Poster Power: Create a poster that illustrates the differences between European art and Chinese art.
- Art Mart: Using illustration 6.11.2, The Painted Word, practice Japanese calligraphy with a brush and ink. Remember that Japanese and Chinese are both written from right to left or from the top to the bottom of the page (Kuiseko 1988, 28–32).
- Poet's Corner: Now using the same illustration (6.11.2), practice writing Japanese Haiku poetry with the same five words translated into English from top to bottom: cloud, color, five, heaven, east. Use the five words to create a beautiful Haiku poem in English. When finished, share your poem with the class and discuss what you have learned about Japanese writing and poetry from this lesson.
- ADV What If?: What if the Christian iconoclasts had dominated in Europe during the Middle Ages? Would calligraphy have become the dominant art form in Europe as it became in the Middle East and in China and Japan?
- ADV Historical Research: How did the development of Chinese and Japanese writing and art focus entirely on the brush—and not the

pen—while European writing and art were clearly separated between the pen and the brush?

- ADV The Futurist: Can there be a moment in time when writing and art merge in the West as they did in China and Japan? What would have to happen first for such a significant historical event to occur?

6.11.3   Beethoven—The Deaf Tone Poet of Bonn, Germany

Ludwig van Beethoven (1770–1827) defined the music of the nineteenth century. He called himself a "tone poet" rather than a musician and he was deaf by the time he was thirty, but that did not stop him from reinventing music. Prior to Beethoven, the music of Mozart, Vivaldi, and others was ambient music to be played for its own beauty before the courts and aristocracy of Europe. Beethoven grew up during the American and French Revolutions with their bold proclamations of liberty for all people. His music reflected these great revolutions both in spirit and audience. His great symphonies written after 1800 were as bold and powerful as the revolutions themselves. He was the first to use the real power of a new instrument—the piano. He was the first to use all the instruments of the full symphony together—strings, percussion, and horns—to produce waves of sound and power. He was the first to use the music of the symphony to produce emotions of sorrow, anger, joy, and happiness rather than just pretty music. He was not just a Romantic, he defined the romanticism of the nineteenth century. The music of the Enlightenment—Mozart, Vivaldi, and Haydn—was controlled, reasonable, and beautiful. The crashing power of Beethoven expressed the raw romantic emotions of the new century. His music was not for the stately courts of Europe, but for all the people liberated during that revolutionary era.

Note from the Future: There is little disagreement among musicians today—Beethoven is considered to be the greatest musician in history. All of the possibilities and feelings expressed by music today would not have existed without the new musical inventions of Beethoven (Boorstin 1992, 452–465).

- Quick Write: Write a short paragraph expressing an emotion of anger, love, or joy. Now imagine a piece of music that would express that emotion. How would it sound? When finished, share your poem and music with the class.

- T Chart: Compare the music of the Enlightenment (Mozart and Vivaldi) with that of the nineteenth century (Beethoven). How are they different from each other?
- Bumper Sticker: Create a pro-Beethoven bumper sticker.
- Counter Spin: Create an anti-Beethoven bumper sticker.
- Tone Poem: Listen to one of Beethoven's symphonies. Create a free verse poem expressing your feelings while you listen to the piece. When finished, share you poem with the class.
- Venn Diagram: Compare your favorite song with a symphony of Beethoven. What are the similarities and differences between them?
- ADV Historical Research: Read about Beethoven and his music in the library. Exactly why is he considered the greatest musician in history?
- ADV Mental Research: Research your library and the Internet to discover exactly how a deaf person like Beethoven can hear and compose great music.
- ADV What if?: What if Beethoven never lived and composed his music? How would music today be different without his contributions?

6.11.4   Oliver Twist, Tiny Tim, and Little Nell

It was a grand love affair—Charles Dickens (1812–1870) and the English public of the nineteenth century. They seemed made for each other. Dickens' England had a new queen—Victoria (1837). It was rapidly building its overseas empire. The new factories of the industrial revolution were polluting the air with coal soot. Illiterate workers were forced to work long hours in unsafe conditions. Ministers, in a Christian revival, preached that hard work and strict morality would have its rewards in heaven. Dickens' father was sent to debtor's prison when Charles was twelve and Charles went to work in a boot-blacking factory where he earned sixty cents (shillings) a week to help support his family. He went to school when he could, but was always taken out when his family could not meet its debts and he was sent back to work at some low-paying job. At the age of seventeen, he became a court reporter and then a journalist. He liked to write about common people— their joys, their sorrows, their aspirations. In 1836, he wrote *The Pickwick Papers* in monthly installments—it expressed the very emotions of the English people around Dickens. The English people on the street

could read and cry or cheer with the characters of Charles Dickens—
Oliver Twist, Tiny Tim, and Little Nell. Very suddenly, Dickens was a
great success—but he did not stop there. He worked throughout his life
to change his stories to fit what the English public wanted. As a result,
his success continued to grow. When he died in 1870, his beloved English public cried at his passing (Boorstin 1992, 364–378).

- Quick Write: In a short paragraph, describe your favorite author.
  Who is your favorite character by this author? Why does this author's
  writing appeal to you?
- Poster Power: Create a poster of one of Dickens' characters—Oliver
  Twist, Tiny Tim, or Little Nell—to rouse the sympathy for the poor
  in nineteenth-century England.
- Role Play: With a partner, create a short skit that depicts the hardships of factory life for the poor during the early industrial revolution
  (a favorite theme of Dickens). When finished, share your skit with
  the class.
- ADV Historical Analysis: Read more about Dickens in your library
  to determine the key factors making Dickens a very popular writer in
  nineteenth-century England and investigate the ways in which he
  worked to retain his popularity.
- ADV The Futurist #1: In teams of four, create a story of poor children today that would raise the consciousness of the country to enact
  legislation intended to help the poor—much as Dickens did in his
  own day.
- ADV The Futurist #2: Find an author today who compares to Dickens during the early nineteenth century. What similarities and differences did you find?
- ADV Personal Plan: If you wanted to become a popular author like
  Charles Dickens, what specific steps would you take in your life to
  develop the writing talent to become such an author and how would
  you retain your popularity once you had obtained it?

6.11.5   Crime and Punishment—The Grand Inquisitor

What is the meaning of life? asked Fyodor Dostoevsky (1821–1881).
Should we search for social causes, as Charles Dickens did with the
poor of England, to seek to improve our lives? No, said Dostoevsky.
Should we turn inward, as Franz Kafka did, and look at the dreams,
memories, fantasies, hopes, and fears that each of us has? No, said Dos-

toevsky. All of these things are Western values of a capitalism that seeks little more than material gain as the goal of life, said Dostoevsky. To improve oneself and to make reasonable decisions, he said from his deeply Russian soul, was to only invite failure and sadness. The duty of every human, said Dostoevsky, was to live in a world in which good and evil exist side by side, very close to each other—the distance between the murderer and the saint is very small. The poor, wretched soul of a human must pick out his path in life in a bewildering panorama of choices and then must live with these decisions. It is this intensely personal freedom to make these hard choices that distinguishes us mortal humans from the animals. In his powerful novels of human passion and striving, such as *Crime and Punishment* and *Brothers Karamazov*, Dostoevsky attacked the center of Western thought—everything from the reason of the Enlightenment to the capitalist view of material gain as the goal of all humans. In its place, Dostoevsky saw a distant and mystical Russian Orthodox God who sat back and laughed at the humans suffering below from the choices—both good and bad—they had made in life.

Note from the Future: Dostoevsky, from his desk in feudal tsarist Russia of the nineteenth century, still remains one of the most powerful novelists the world has produced and his novels remain as major critiques of Western values and ideals (Boorstin 1992, 658–671).

- Quick Write: In a short paragraph, describe a choice you once made that had terrible consequences. What did you do to improve the results of your bad decision? (This is a typical problem for a character in a Dostoevsky novel.)
- Bumper Sticker: Create a bumper sticker illustrating Dostoevsky's basic problem of freedom of choice.
- Poster Power: Create a poster reflecting Dostoevsky's critique of Western values.
- Pair Share: With a partner, discuss the basic elements of Dostoevsky's critique of Western values and whether or not you agree with them. When finished, present your views to the class.
- Meet the Press: As host of this popular TV show during the nineteenth century, have the reporters gathered today (students in class) prepare a list of questions to ask Dostoevsky, who has graciously accepted to take a time machine into the future. Dostoevsky (a well-prepared student or teacher in costume) may then respond to reporters' questions.

- ADV Historical Research: What in Dostoevsky's background in Russia makes him able to come up with such a different view of life from all of Europe during the Enlightenment and from the growing materialist views of the nineteenth century?

6.11.6 Wagner—The Dark Side of Romanticism

"Tutto nel mondo e burla" (All the world's a joke) said Verdi in the last line of his opera *Falstaff*. Richard Wagner (1813–1883) was a direct opposite of Verdi's Falstaff. Wagner took the world very seriously—too seriously. He was a student who saw Beethoven as his musical idol; he was also a political revolutionary who participated in the abortive workers' revolution of 1849 in Dresden and was forced to flee Germany. He believed in uniting all the arts—writing, music, and dance—into the single art form of grand opera—and spent his lifetime seeking to create the perfect opera. He was also a very serious German nationalist who believed in the "Das Volk"—the spirit of the German people. The grand opera he composed, *Der Ring des Nibelungen*, centered on the mythological origins of the German people in four parts—*Das Rheingold, Die Walküre, Siegfried,* and *Götterdämmerung*. Wagner's gigantic four-day operatic masterpiece was first performed together in 1876. Very little about Wagner was light, happy, and joking; his opera and music are the heavyweight, extreme expressions of musical emotion of the romantic era started by Beethoven. Unfortunately, his legacy for the future also includes his vicious anti-Jewish bigotry. Wagner's bigotry is strange because he might have come from a Jewish background and some of the major people who supported him in his education as a musician were Jewish.

Note from the Future: The darkest chapter in the history of Wagner, however, happened after his death. The Nazi Party of Adolf Hitler made Wagner the patron saint of their cause in the twentieth century, which combined the extreme German nationalism of Wagner with his anti-Jewish bigotry, to produce two of history's great tragedies—World War II and the Jewish Holocaust (Boorstin 1992, 476–486).

- Quick Write: In a short paragraph, give a description of what you think the end of the world might be like.
- Poster Power: Draw a picture advertising Wagner's opera *Die Walküre* (The Valkyries), large, mythological female warriors with horned helmets who carry dead German soldiers to heaven.

- Opera Buff: Listen to Wagner's *Die Walküre* (for a few minutes—this is pretty heavy stuff) and imagine in your mind the Valkyries carrying off the fallen dead. Create a short dramatic poem that depicts this scene.
- ADV Psychological Research: Research in the library why a person becomes a bigot against a certain ethnic group—especially when that person might have been from that ethnic group.
- ADV The Futurist #1: Research in the library how the Nazi Party of the twentieth century combined the fanatical German nationalism of Wagner with his anti-Jewish bigotry to create propaganda for their movement.
- ADV The Futurist #2: Examine events in today's news that parallel Wagner's combining extreme nationalism with bigotry against a particular ethnic group.

6.12.0   SUCCESSES AND FAILURES OF THE ERA

6.12.1   Abolition of the Slave Trade (1807)

Europe at the beginning of the nineteenth century no longer needed slaves. Due to better food supplies as a result of the agricultural revolution, the population of Europe was rapidly increasing. The growing industrialization of Europe also meant that fewer laborers were needed. Corresponding to these economic changes, an abolitionist movement of Christian evangelists began to have its impact across Europe. In 1788, *Le Société des Amis de Noires* (The Society of the Friends of Blacks) in France began to push for the abolition of the slave trade and in 1794 succeeded in making French citizens of all slaves in French colonies. In England, William Wilberforce (1759–1833) and the Clapham Sect led Parliament to abolish the slave trade in 1807. All European countries, with the exception of Russia, followed these examples by abolishing the slave trade in 1815 at the Congress of Vienna. In the United States, it took a Civil War to force the southern states to abolish slavery in 1865 (Palmer 1974, 27).

- Quick Write: In a short paragraph, describe what it might feel like to be bought and sold as a slave with no rights.
- Graffiti: On a large piece of paper, scrawl a pro-abolitionist slogan from the nineteenth century to place up on your classroom wall.

- Music Mart: With a partner, create a poem, song, or rap that supports the abolitionist movement.
- Time Line: Research the abolitionist movement in your school library and create a time line from its beginnings to the final abolition of the slave trade and slavery across the world. Present the time line to your class and display it along your classroom wall.
- Poster Power: Create a poster illustrating the forces coming together at the beginning of the nineteenth century that led to the abolition of the slave trade and slavery.
- Drama Team: In groups of four, create a short skit that illustrates the struggle to abolish the slave trade.
- ADV Sociological Research: Research the impact on a society when it enslaves part of its population.
- ADV The Futurist: Research the negative impact slavery had on the development of the United States as a nation.

6.12.2   The Opium Wars (1839–1842)

"Barbarian" traders from Europe before 1800 had a great deal of difficulty conducting business with China—Europe wanted tea and silk in large quantities from China, but China did not want anything from Europe. The trade balance, as a result, was always in favor of China. All of this changed suddenly after 1800. The English started manufacturing the drug opium in large quantities in India. One of the major markets for this opium was China. British merchants from India began to ship opium to China in large quantities. Large numbers of Chinese became addicted to the drug and suddenly the traditional trade balance shifted in favor of England. The government of the Manchu emperor became alarmed and quickly banned the import of any more opium into China. As with all bans, this one was bypassed with widespread smuggling. The Chinese government began to directly confiscate and burn any opium it found in China—including that still in British hands. The British responded in 1839 with naval attacks to force China to buy the opium it was selling. After several attacks by British warships, the Chinese emperor reluctantly signed the Treaty of Nanking in 1842, which formally gave Hong Kong, and several other ports, to the British and recognized the British monarch as equal to the celestial emperor. The Opium Wars were the beginning of the end of the Celestial Empire of China. European "barbarians" for the first time were allowed to control parts of China—the most valuable ports in the country. The recognition that other people were equal to the Chinese also disrupted the calm Confucian philosophy of superiority that had ruled China for so long. The relinquishing of China's most valuable ports to foreigners also severely limited China's ability to become a fully modern nation of the world during the nineteenth and twentieth centuries (Liao 1984; Michael 1986, 168–174).

- Quick Write: In a short paragraph, describe an instance in your life when you were forced to do something you did not want to do. What happened as a result of this incident?
- Bumper Sticker #1: Create a Chinese bumper sticker protesting against the British in 1839.
- Bumper Sticker #2: Create a pro-British bumper sticker against the Chinese in 1839.
- T Chart: Create a T chart that distinguishes between the British and Chinese viewpoints during the Opium Wars.
- Poster Power: On a poster, illustrate the tremendous changes that eventually took place in China as a result of the Opium Wars.
- Front Page: With a team of four student editors, create a front-page edition of the *Industrial Times* newspaper on the Treaty of Nanking in 1842. Be sure to interview a British naval officer who was at Nanking and a representative of the emperor of China and have them describe the impact of the treaty on China. Do they think China should be modernized and open to world trade, or retain its traditional isolation as the Celestial Empire and closed to the outside world?
- ADV Historical Analysis: Compare China after the Opium Wars (1842) and Japan after Commodore Perry's gunboat diplomacy (1853) (see TLP 5.12.3). How were the two provocations similar to each other and how were the responses of the two countries different from each other? (Hint: one country was stimulated into action and modernization; the other was stimulated into action but fell apart.)
- ADV The Futurist: Find examples when other countries deliberately encouraged the sale of drugs, as England did during the Opium Wars. What happened to these countries as a result of these immoral actions?

6.12.3   Perry Opens Japan (1853)

In 1853, one of the last acts of Millard Fillmore, a rather ineffective president of the United States, was to send Commodore Matthew Perry to

Japan with a weak letter requesting the emperor of Japan to open Japan to trade with the United States. This letter from Fillmore was a small, first step toward the continued westward expansion of the United States beyond California, which had just become part of the United States in 1850. It was also an early step by the United States to demonstrate that it was becoming an industrialized world power with steam-powered warships and was interested in imperial expansion—just like England and France. Three centuries before, feudal Japan, always fearful of foreigners, had cut off all foreign trade and contact—except with China and minor contact with the Portuguese and Dutch in Nagasaki. Perry decided he really did not like Fillmore's letter to the Japanese emperor—it was too weak. By the time Perry reached Japan, Fillmore was out of power in the United States, and Perry took advantage of this historical time loop and wrote his own forceful letter to the Japanese emperor, demanding that Japan open trade with the United States. When Perry's four black, steam-powered warships reached Tokyo harbor, Perry handed both letters to the emperor and stated he would return the following year with eight black, steam-driven warships to demand the emperor's answer. All of Japan was impressed and frightened by these new black, steam-powered warships of the industrial revolution. Perry was true to his word and returned in 1854 with eight threatening warships within striking distance of the emperor's palace. Very quickly and fearfully, the Japanese agreed to the opening of trade to American ships. Many in the Japanese government also realized that Japan, if it was going to retain its independence, would have to rapidly move from its self-imposed feudalism of the Middle Ages to a modern nineteenth-century state.

Note from the Future: The Meiji Restoration in a few short years would move Japan quickly toward modernization and fully into the nineteenth century, with the power to conquer most of Asia for a short time during the early twentieth century (Palmer 1974, 147–153).

- Quick Write: Think back to a period in your life when you wish that you had said something, but then later wish you had stated it a different way. Write a short paragraph describing the incident and share it with the class.
- Poster Power: Create a poster that illustrates the way you think the Japanese saw Perry's battleships in 1853 sitting in Tokyo harbor.
- Map It: On a blank map of the world, illustrate the imperialistic direction of the United States to continue its expansion westward across the Pacific.

- T Chart: Compare the thinking of Japan and the United States in 1853 in regard to international trade.
- You Were There: As the host of this popular nineteenth-century TV program, have the members of your studio audience (students from the class) each prepare three questions to ask of the following guests (well-prepared students in costume) to your show:
  1. Captain Merlin Tutmuffin—the captain of one of Perry's steam-powered warships
  2. Himoto Nakura—a traditional Japanese samurai soldier who wants nothing to do with the Americans
  3. Irving Lovejoy—a young American missionary on Perry's warship who came to Japan to convert the Japanese to Christianity and the American way of life
  4. Mitsu Hirohonshu—a modern advisor to the Japanese emperor who saw the need for Japan to quickly adapt Western ways before being conquered by either the United States or another European power
- ADV Historical Analysis: Using your library for research, trace the change in American attitudes toward Japan from a strange foreign country in 1853 to a strong racist bigotry against the Japanese during the early to mid-twentieth century.

(Other TLPs to see: 6.4.2 on the Meiji Restoration and 7.7.2 Japan's Hundred Year War.)

6.13.0 MAJOR HISTORICAL PROBLEMS IN RETROSPECT

6.13.1 The Ecological Results of the Industrial Revolution

More food was produced by the agricultural revolution of the eighteenth and nineteenth centuries in Europe and America than at any other time in history. Better farming tools and more land placed under cultivation resulted in more food being produced. Large landholders ejected poor peasant farmers off common land. The large landholders, in turn, could now produce more food more efficiently. The poor peasant farmers migrated to the cities to become the workers of the industrial revolution. More food for everyone, however, resulted in a large increase in the population. The larger population, in turn, created a larger demand for more food. The intense overuse of land for growing crops, however, created new problems. It led to the depletion of vital minerals in the soil (such as nitrogen) that are essential for good crop production. The more the farmers planted on the depleted soil, the fewer the crops the farmers could harvest. (Economists call this "diminishing returns.") Across Europe and America, between 1830 and 1870, a major problem was the depletion of the soil. The result of this depletion was either the abandoning of the land in order to move to more productive land or the addition of fertilizer to the soil. To remedy the second situation, the first boatload of Peruvian guano arrived in England in 1835 and the first artificial fertilizer was introduced in 1842. In the United States, one of the major crises that led to the Civil War was caused by the cotton plantation owners in the South when they depleted the soil and wanted to open new western lands to cotton growing and more slavery. It was during this time of soil depletion during the nineteenth century that Thomas Malthus created his doomsday theory that overpopulation and soil depletion would eventually lead to starvation and misery across the world. Karl Marx, however, was more optimistic. He saw that soil depletion and overpopulation could both be eliminated by everyone working in common for a balanced, sustainable agriculture rather than exploitation and depletion of the land by few large landowners (Foster and Magdoff 1998, 32–45).

- Quick Write: In a short paragraph, describe what you think would happen if too many deer are grazing a small amount of parkland. Make a list of possible remedies to the situation, and then pick the remedy that you think is the best.
- Poster Power: Create a nineteenth-century bumper sticker supporting one of the following positions:
  1. L. T. Wacko—a prophet of doom who says the end of the world is near because the soil is being depleted
  2. B. G. Blowhard—a large capitalist landowner who says that all the stories about soil depletion are not true, and that he has just purchased enough new farmland in Australia to feed everybody
  3. Thomas Malthus—the theorist who calls for limits to population growth to have enough food for all
  4. Lester Goodsmell—a fertilizer salesman who says that bat guano is the best fertilizer to improve crops
  5. Karl Marx—the revolutionary who calls for a sustainable agriculture owned by everyone together rather than private landholders

- Poster Power: Create a poster that illustrates the cycle of problems brought on by the agricultural revolution: more food, more people, more use of the land, soil depletion, and starvation.
- Poet's Corner: Compose a short epic poem of the ecological joys and sorrows of the agricultural revolution during the nineteenth century.
- You Were There: As the host of this popular TV program during the nineteenth century, have the members of your studio audience (students in class) write down three questions to ask each of our guests on the ecological problems of the nineteenth century. (Use the same list as above: the prophet of doom, the large capitalist landowner— complete with cigar, Malthus, the fertilizer salesman, and Marx.) The program may be taped for later broadcast.
- ADV Historical Analysis: Use your library to research the problem of soil depletion and overpopulation throughout history. How many people have been forced to emigrate, have caused wars, or have ended major civilizations due to these factors (for example: the ancient Mayans)?
- ADV The Futurist: Examine the problems of soil depletion and overpopulation in a given country in the world. Are they still major problems in areas like China? What actions have governments and farmers done to combat these problems? What actions need to be taken in the future to solve these problems?

6.13.2   Pollution and Microbes

Epidemic disease has plagued humans ever since people started living in towns. No one knew what caused the diseases or how to prevent them. People were terrified of epidemic diseases such as smallpox, cholera, and the bubonic plague, and most often treated them with a combination of praying, magic potions, quarantines, and burning of objects associated with the sick person. The industrial revolution, with its accompanying large immigration into towns, amplified this problem far beyond anything ever seen by humankind. Garbage and human waste were commonly just thrown in the streets. The runoff of this waste flowed into a river. People downstream then obtained their drinking water from the same river. One of the world's first "sanitarians" (as they were called) was Edwin Chadwick, who believed that urban cleanliness was a major means of preventing epidemic diseases. A terrible cholera epidemic attacked London in 1848 and convinced the British government to act on Chadwick's recommendations. A General Board of Health for the City of London, a system of pipes for bringing pure water to the city, and a sewage disposal system were all established. The other major cities of Europe and America quickly began to follow London's sanitation example. Louis Pasteur of France and Robert Koch of Germany quickly added scientific support to Chadwick's sanitation recommendations with their study of microbes (small living organisms) as the cause of epidemic diseases. Sanitation plus the vaccines to guard against such microbes greatly reduced the danger of major epidemic diseases in large industrial towns. In the space of only a few years, the death rate from an epidemic disease such as typhoid dropped from 332 per million in 1871 to 35 per million in 1911 in the industrialized world (Burchell 1966, 36–37).

- Quick Write: In a short paragraph, describe an instance in your life when you encountered unsanitary conditions such as polluted water or improper disposal of waste. What happened as a result of this unsanitary condition?
- Bumper Sticker: Create a bumper sticker that Chadwick could have used to promote sanitation in nineteenth-century London.
- Counter Spin: Create a bumper sticker for nineteenth-century London that favors less governmental control and more pollution.
- T Chart: With a partner, create a T chart that lists a major source of urban pollution on one side and the means of stopping this pollution on the other side.
- Poster Power: Create a poster that illustrates the difference in city living that Chadwick introduced to city governments across the industrial world.
- Quick Skit: In a team of four, create a short skit demonstrating the immense problems of pollution that came with the rapid urbanization of the nineteenth century and how Chadwick's ideas helped solve this problem.
- ADV Historical Analysis: Use your library to research how the ancient Indus River civilization and ancient Rome handled massive urban pollution problems such as unclean water and sewage, and compare their efforts with those of Chadwick in nineteenth-century England. When finished, report your findings to your class.
- ADV The Futurist #1: Survey your own community for sources of pollution and then find out from your local government what is being done about these sources of pollution.

- ADV The Futurist #2: Using a Venn diagram, compare the urban pollution and epidemic disease problems of nineteenth-century England with those the world faces today.
- ADV The Futurist #3: In a team of four, make a list of current major pollution and epidemic disease problems faced by the world today. Rank these major problems in order of importance. When finished, pick out one major pollution or epidemic disease problem and create a plan to actively control it.

6.13.3   Militaristic Nationalism

The dream of building a nation fired the romantic imagination of individuals in ethnic groups across Europe during the first half of the nineteenth century. This romantic call for a national state also swept across Germany with a passion, but Germany in 1860 still consisted of thirty-nine separate states ruled by princes, dukes, and petty kings. Otto von Bismarck (1815–1898) was an aristocratic Prussian with no romantic views for a German national state or any wish for democratic government. He was foremost a Prussian authoritarian who wanted "blood and iron," not democracy. As the minister-president of Prussia in 1862, he immediately worked to create a German empire (*reich*) dominated by Prussia. While other Germans dreamed about a national state, Bismarck quickly modernized the Prussian army with a well-trained high command, the latest weapons, and the best railways in Europe. Using the weakest of excuses, Bismarck quickly conquered several small German states and through intimidation convinced the rest of Germany to accept the Prussian rule. In 1871, Bismarck declared that the German empire was under his leadership. Bismarck tricked the nationalistic German democrats into accepting the autocratic rule of Prussia by giving them the national state they wanted, and also the right to have everybody vote for representatives in the German parliament. The German parliament, however, had no real power. The new unified German nation, instead of being a democratic state, was ruled by a Prussian emperor, a Prussian military, and above all, a Prussian named Bismarck. The dream of a democratic nation rapidly changed into a national state whose military power could quickly crush any rebellion and could force its will on any weaker neighboring states. Darwin's "survival of the fittest" was now the motto of the new nation-states of Europe. With it, they could justify the violence they used against other weaker neighboring states and justify their colonial expansion across the rest of the world (Burchell 1966, 96–106).

- Quick Write: Write a short paragraph describing a time when you were bullied by someone to do something you did not want to do. What happened as a result?
- Bumper Sticker: Create a bumper sticker to either support or oppose Prussian dominance over the rest of Germany in 1871.
- Poster Power: Create a poster illustrating the methods by which Bismarck brought Germany under Prussian domination.
- Pros and Cons: Create a dialogue between two Germans discussing whether or not to accept Bismarck's forcing German unification.
- T Chart: Compare the romantic views of nationalism before Bismarck and the militaristic nationalism after Bismarck.
- Role Play: In a team of four, create a short role-play that demonstrates the different perspectives of the new militaristic national state of Germany:
  1. Reinhart Geldsmertz—a romantic poet who dreams of a unified democratic German state
  2. Adolf von Pomfritz—a proud aristocratic German army officer
  3. Duke Otto von Freiling—a duke in a small German state next to Prussia
  4. Luigi Bocherini—a non-German worker in a Prussian gun factory
- ADV The Futurist: In your library, research the bloody impact of the growing European militaristic nationalism on the twentieth century.

6.14.0   NINETEENTH-CENTURY ANTECEDENTS FOR THE FUTURE

6.14.1   What Is the Shape of History?

What was the shape of history during the nineteenth century—straight lines, circles, or curved lines?

- Poster Power: Make a poster illustrating the shape of history according to your reading, discussion, and understanding of the nineteenth century.

6.14.2   Great Symbols of Political and Religious Power

The Egyptian pyramids were the great symbols of political or religious power during the classical period of history. What were the great symbols of political power during the nineteenth century?

Art Share: With a partner, draw a picture of what you think was a major symbol of political or religious power during the nineteenth century and compare it to the symbols of power in other eras. Present your drawing to the class.

6.14.3   The Economic Revolution of the Nineteenth Century

During the nineteenth century, Europe was transformed from small feudal states into large national states. Large industrial companies supported by their strong national governments began to dominate the economy of Europe and spread across the world. Nobles and the Church were no longer major economic factors during the nineteenth century. Capitalism, however, was a major factor in the economies of Europe and the United States.

- Role Play: Transform your classroom into a nineteenth-century town, with each student presenting the former noble rulers, evangelistic churchmen, the rich capitalist factory owners, the powerful merchants in town, factory workers, romantic poets and musicians, and impressionist artists. Create a small drama in which all participants take part—Jack, a factory mechanic's son, has called for workers to be given equal rights by the factory owners and wants to marry the factory owner's daughter, Mildred. Shocking! What will happen? Let everyone take part in this free-flow, nineteenth-century drama and see what happens.
- ADV Comparative Research: Compare the imperialistic capitalism of the nineteenth century with the feudalism of the Middle Ages and the capitalism of the late twentieth century and early twenty-first century.

6.14.4   The Spark of Historical Change

Major changes in world history are often not caused by major events. The change of thinking during the nineteenth century was caused by romantic writers and poets describing new ethnic nations and by thinkers creating the relatively small inventions of the agricultural and industrial revolutions. None of them foresaw the major bloodshed the new militaristic national states would bring in the twentieth century and the flood of new ideas and thinking that would bring on the technological and informational revolutions of the twentieth century.

Note from the Future: Be on the lookout throughout history and in the future for small new ideas or event that can lead major changes in history.

- Quick List: Make a list of small, new ideas in your lifetime— different from the ones at the end of the nineteenth century—that have led to major changes in the world.
- Historical Hypothesis: Pick out another major historical change in your lifetime and hypothesize what would have happened if this change had not taken place.
- ADV Pattern Seeking: Go back through history to find the initial cause of major changes in history. How many of these initial causes were very small and insignificant?

6.14.5   Endpoint of the Nineteenth Century/Start of the Twentieth Century

The following are research questions to answer about the end of the nineteenth century and the beginning of the twentieth century:

- ADV Nineteenth-Century Analysis #1: Many things were happening before 1900 that led to the changes during the twentieth century. Pick a year that you think best represents the end of the nineteenth century and the beginning of the twentieth century and defend why you think that is the changeover date. (Reality Note: Even historians cannot agree on a date for this change.)
- ADV Nineteenth-Century Analysis #2: Who are the key individuals whose thinking during the nineteenth century transforms the world as the twentieth century emerges? What are their key ideas that affect the future?

6.14.6   Is Humankind Ready to Advance?

It is now time to judge whether or not humankind is ready to advance into the next era. Five members from around Industrial Town (the class) will state their basic viewpoints whether or not humankind has advanced enough. The five illustrious members are as follows:
  1. Burtran Limdunk, the archconservative of Industrial Town, who believes that humankind has gone far enough with enough

progress. Burtran believes strongly that the good old days were the best and that humankind needs to hold strongly to past values and beliefs.

2. Ruby Deru, one of the rising young voices in the town, is a more moderate conservative who believes that we need to be very cautious with any change and be very sure that no harm will come to Industrial Town if change takes place. Ruby is willing to accept some change, but only in very small amounts and only when the time is right—and wants to be the one to decide when that time will come.

3. Louie Wookwam, the wishy-washy middle-of-the-roader around the town, is willing to accept change for a few minutes after one speaker, but may have a change of mind in an instant to oppose change after another speaker has finished.

4. Ludwig Vatsmeer, the moderate progressive of the group is willing to support change for the good of the people in Industrial Town. Vatsmeer is especially in favor of change when it will benefit Vatsmeer's own family directly.

5. Karl Varull, the radical progressive of the town, is very willing to support any change that will move humanity away from a drafty and leaky basement apartment into something more modern and comfortable for humanity.

- Members of Industrial Town (classroom) now must chose one of the five positions for humanity and to take and support the position with evidence of what they have learned about the nineteenth century.

- A vote will then be taken of all factory owners and workers around town to determine whether or not humanity should move on to the next era. The consensus decision of the imaginary citizens of Industrial Town will determine their own future and the rest of humanity. (In reality, such decisions by people during the nineteenth century were key in deciding whether humans stayed the way they were or progressed to new levels of development.)

The Twentieth Century

UNIT 7: TABLE OF CONTENTS

INTRODUCTION TO THE TWENTIETH CENTURY

The twentieth century was an age of accelerating scientific knowledge and inventions; computers, television, airplanes, rockets, and cellular telephones rapidly changed the way humans think and live. Certainly, the most important discovery of the twentieth century was the awesome quantum nature of our universe as explored by Einstein, Heisenberg, and Bohr. These quantum discoveries pushed aside Newton's simple machine model of cause and effect regarding how our universe operates, and replaced it with a unified, interdependent, and ever-changing universe of interacting relationships. Humanity during the twentieth century, however, was still comfortable with its simple machine model of the universe and refused to accept the new quantum tenets of an interdependent world. Instead of becoming more interdependent and unified, many of the peoples of the world used their new scientific knowledge to create new and better weapons to fight each other. More major wars, conflicts, and acts of gross inhumanity were committed during this century than in all of human history combined. At the beginning of the century, England was the dominant country in the world and Europe was the dominant continent, but this quickly changed with Europe's foolhardy plunge into World War I (1914–1918). The war killed off a whole generation of Europe's best young men. The political vacuum left by Europe after World War I was slowly filled by the United States. The United States, comfortable behind the safety of its oceans, slowly and reluctantly emerged as the major power in the world. By the end of World War II (1945), the United States was clearly the major political, economic, and military power in the world. The preoccupation of the United States after 1945, however, was with the communist dictatorship of Joseph Stalin in the USSR. The result was an extended period of friction (1945–1990) between the United States and the USSR. This strange "Cold War" threatened to destroy life on this planet in a cloud of radioactive dust particles—which thankfully never happened. The Cold War ended almost as strangely as it began. In 1991, the USSR, weakened by decades of ineffective leadership, dissolved itself into separate national states. Even still, by the end of the twentieth century, the United States and the rest of the world had not come to grips with the interdependent nature of its new quantum universe: wars and acts of intolerance were still endemic between the peoples of the world. The realization of the interdependent nature of the world remains the major task for humanity in the twenty-first century.

THEMATIC LESSON PACS FOR THE TWENTIETH CENTURY

7.1.0   HISTORICAL TIME LINE

7.1.1   Twentieth-Century Time Line

- Name Plates: Photocopy six sets of the fourteen names and items below. Cut each name or item into a strip of paper. Place the strips of paper carefully into separate envelopes for each team and label the envelopes "7.1.1 Twentieth-Century History Chain" for later use in class.
- Group Power: Break the class into six teams.
- The Envelope: Each team should be given an envelope containing the following random fourteen names from the twentieth century:
  1. Lindbergh flew across the Atlantic (1927)
  2. Panama Canal built (1903)
  3. Humans on the moon (1969)
  4. Russian Revolution (1917)
  5. Mao's Long March (1934)
  6. Wright brothers' airplane (1903)
  7. Transistor invented (1947)
  8. Rise of Adolf Hitler and the Nazis in Germany (1933)
  9. The Great Depression started (1929)
  10. The collapse of the Soviet Union (1991)
  11. Versailles Conference (1919)
  12. Marconi's first radio transmission (1901)
  13. United Nations founded (1944)
  14. Heisenberg's uncertainty principle (1927)
- Team Time Line: The first job of each team is to correctly order the fourteen names and artifacts according to time, with the oldest at the top and the most recent at the bottom. Each student should separately write the correct time line for the twentieth century names and artifacts on a personal sheet of paper for later reference.

- Team Look Up: Once every member of the team has his or her own twentieth-century time line on a sheet of paper, each of the fourteen twentieth-century names should be divided between members of the team to find out the meaning of each name from the textbook. Once found, the meaning of each twentieth-century name can be shared with the members of the team to write on their own time lines.
- Poster Power: On a large piece of paper, each team should construct its own time line for the twentieth century using the fourteen names and including descriptions and illustrations to demonstrate the meaning of each name. When finished, these can be presented to the class and displayed on the classroom wall.
- Music Mart: Teams should pick what they think is the most important name or event in the time line and then compose a short song or rap about the name or event. When finished, this can be presented to the class for their approval.
- Journal Entry: Team members should write a short journal entry speculating about what they now know about the development of humans during the twentieth century and possibly the most important things to happen during this era. When finished, students can first share their thoughts with their teams and then with the class as a whole for general discussion about what they think are the most important things that happened during the era.

7.2.0   SEPARATING FACT FROM MYTH AND PROPAGANDA

7.2.1   *Heart of Darkness* (1902)

Polish writer Joseph Conrad wrote his starkly graphic novel *Heart of Darkness* in 1902. In the novel, Marlow, an innocent ship's captain, takes his boat up the Congo (Lualaba) River in Africa to find Kurtz, who is nobly bringing "civilization" to the people. Conrad wrote his novel as a dark parody of human relations in the European and American colonies created just before the beginning of the twentieth century in Africa. Europeans and Americans spoke nobly of their conquests of Africa to bring "civilization" to the people of Africa, but Conrad in his travels as a seaman witnessed a much crueler colonialism. In King Leopold's Belgian Congo, African women and children were held captive without food until their men could bring back a set quota of wild rubber to sell to the Europeans and Americans, who needed the rubber to make the tires for that

IN THE RUBBER COILS.

Illustration 7.2.1 *The "Civilizing" of Africa*

new invention, the automobile. As the rubber became scarcer and the men had to travel further to find less rubber, less food was grown and millions of Congolese people starved to death. The title of Conrad's tale—*Heart of Darkness*—clearly did not just refer to the skin color of the people of Africa, but to the cruel hoax of the heart of the "civilizing" mission of the European and American colonies (Hochschild 1998).

- Quick Write: Take a moment and think of an example of a person who said that they were really doing good, but in reality were doing something quite bad. Write a short paragraph describing your example and then share it with the class.
- Map Attack: Using a historical atlas, indicate on a blank map of the world the location of the Congo or Lualaba River—the site of the story *Heart of Darkness*—and then on the same map indicate the major colonies controlled by England, France, Germany, Belgium, Portugal, and the United States around the year 1900.
- You Were There: As hosts of that most popular TV program of the twentieth century *You Were There,* have your studio audience ask questions of four guests who witnessed the colonial experience of the early twentieth century. Your four guests (students in costume) are as follows:

1. Lord Mountburp—the colonial governor of several European colonies in Africa for many years. He loves to give speeches about the "civilizing" mission of Europe in educating the rest of the world to think like Europeans. He also became quite rich during his stay in Africa by growing crops quite cheaply and selling them to Europe at quite high prices.
2. Reverent Lompast—a missionary who carried the word of the Christian God and Western civilization to unbelievers across the world in many European colonies. The good reverend strongly believes that everyone in the world should have the same religious beliefs as the good people in Europe.
3. Jomo Kendata—an African who was educated by European missionaries and received a doctorate in anthropology from a major European university. Dr. Kendata is quite angry that many Europeans and Americans believe that colonialism is good for Africa. He sees colonialism as a means for the Europeans to steal the valuable minerals and crops of Africa at a cheap price and get little or nothing in return.
4. Fuziwe Kraai—a traditional storyteller and poet of Africa who sees many benefits from European colonialism but many more of its negative influences on the continent. Learning European reading and writing were useful, she thinks, but being forced to live under European rule for almost sixty years was insulting and did not train young African men and women in how to govern countries democratically.

- Poster Power: Create a poster that illustrates the contradictions of European colonialism illustrated in Conrad's *Heart of Darkness*.
- ADV Research #1: Read Conrad's *Heart of Darkness* and then report to your class on your impression of the book and the European colonialism of Africa it that portrayed.
- ADV Research #2: Review current news articles on Africa from European and American newspapers and television. From your analysis of these European and American current news sources, how much of Conrad's portrayal of European and American colonial attitudes toward Africa still exist? What has to happen to change these attitudes?

7.2.2   Leni Riefenstahl (1934)

One of the most controversial documentary films ever produced was *Triumph of the Will*, produced in 1934 by a thirty-three-year-old female film director by the name of Leni Riefenstahl. Riefenstahl focused on the building of a Nordic mythology around Hitler using the new medium of film. The film opens with Hitler's airplane descending out of the clouds and glistening sun, with the triumphal sounds of Wagner's *Flight of the Valkyries* playing in the background. The airplane door opens revealing the godlike Hitler to the adoring masses of his party supporters. Above them all is Hitler, his arm stretched out, saluting the one million party loyalists below him. Hitler is triumphant. He is the god that all Germans have been waiting for. Riefenstahl's film, even today, is considered a masterpiece of propaganda and a model for other such film efforts in the future. Certainly Hitler is considered to be one of the most evil men of the twentieth century, but Riefenstahl transformed this image of evil into a godlike savior for the German people. Riefenstahl was never a Nazi, and still insists today that she was just hired to produce a film about the Nazis. She denies any responsibility for the millions of young Germans who were recruited into the Nazi Party by the inspiration they received from Riefenstahl's masterpiece of propaganda.

- Quick Write: In a short paragraph, give a description of advertising (propaganda) you have seen that makes something that is really *not* very good into something that looks like it *is* really something very good. When finished, share your description with the class.
- Pair Share: With a partner, think of a popular piece of advertising today and then identify one technique you think advertisers used in this ad to make someone or something look much better than it really is. The class can then share the techniques they have identified with the class for further discussion.
- Master Propagandists: In teams of four students, have each team develop a thirty-second TV jingle to make a rather bad political candidate appear to be exactly what the people want using the propaganda techniques below:
  Propaganda Techniques (to deliberately influence a group of people to change their attitudes toward a person, thing, or another group of people):
  1. Focus on an emotional symbol: a flag, a religious symbol, a devoted mother, a sad child, a patriotic soldier.
  2. Embellish the truth: Take a basic fact or idea and stretch, twist, and spin it to suit your own needs.

3. Agitation: Deliberately build up the emotions of the viewers or listeners in sadness, happiness, or anger.

4. Reinforcement: Repeat a lie often enough to make it sound true.

5. Commitment: Convince the viewers or listeners to act on the propaganda just given them.

- Poster Power: Using the propaganda techniques illustrated above, create a poster that is designed to convince young men to be patriotic, fight for, and perhaps die for their country.

- Positive Spin: Take a piece of news from a current newspaper and "spin" this news in four different directions of propaganda:

  1. To make the news appear favorable
  2. To make the news appear negative
  3. To make it appear favorable to a political or religious cause
  4. To make it appear negative to a political or religious cause

- ADV Research #1: The word propaganda originally comes from the Catholic Church after the Reformation around 1519 and was used to influence its church members to stay in the Church. Read from sources in the library and on the Internet about how effective propaganda has been in influencing people in history.

- ADV Research #2: Critically examine the news for one day on the front page of a newspaper or a news broadcast on TV and try to determine—using the above criteria—how often propaganda might have been used to deliberately influence people.

- Action Research: Conduct discussions in class with parents, neighbors, and friends on how we can lessen the wide use of propaganda in our news media today. Create a deliberate plan of action based on these discussions to correct this major problem in our society.

7.2.3   *Wag the Dog* (1998)

Does the dog wag its tail, or does the tail wag the dog? Sometimes, in the politics of the late twentieth century, we can never be too sure. In the 1998 film (staring Robert DeNiro, Anne Heche, and Dustin Hoffman), a president needs to raise his popularity at the polls for the upcoming election. A Hollywood movie director is hired to stage a short "fake" war with Albania, with fake war heroes. The president's popularity goes up. He wins the election due to the popularity of the "fake" war.

With the knowledge that some of the information we receive in the newspapers and television is false, how can we spot when the information "spin" (the tail) is wagging the dog (the government)? Answer: We must view all information we receive with intelligent skepticism and verify it against other international sources. If the news sounds too good, or the television news looks too patriotic and appealing to personal human values, we need to be suspicious of its authenticity. The tail may be wagging the dog again.

- Quick Write: Think back over the past weeks to a piece of news that you thought might be suspicious. Write a short paragraph describing the piece of news and why you thought it was suspicious.
- T Chart: With a partner, look at a recent piece of news in the newspaper and place each step of the news item down the left side of the T chart. On the right hand side of the T chart, create a "spin" on the news (tail) that changes the whole interpretation of the news.
- Front Page: In a team of four student editors, create a front-page edition of the *Digital Times*—the cyberspace newspaper of the twentieth century—in which a recent news event is completely changed around to make someone appear more positive.
- Quick Skit: In a team of four, create a short dramatization of taking a recent historical event and changing the "spin" on it so the "tail wags the dog" in favor of someone else.
- Poster Power: Create a poster that illustrates how the tail can wag the dog in a recent historical incident.
- ADV Research: Go back in history and identify events that sound suspiciously like the winners of a particular historical incident "wagged the dog" to make themselves appear more favorable in the eyes of future historians.

7.3.0 LOCATION AND MOVEMENT

7.3.1 The Lunatic Express—1901

Politicians in any government can make incredibly crazy decisions based on what they consider to be the best information available. One such crazy decision was the building of the Uganda Railway by the British government—started in 1895 and finished in 1901. By 1895, England had the world's largest colonial empire and Uganda was about as far from anywhere as possible and was fairly inconsequential. It was in the middle of Africa at the headwaters of the White Nile River and

Lake Victoria, as well as being hundreds of miles from the Indian Ocean. Someone in the British Colonial Office, perhaps with nothing better to do, started looking at a map of Africa and realized that Egypt—the location of the Suez Canal—was totally dependent for water on the Nile River. Well, daydreamed the colonial officer, what if the French should grab Uganda, dam the Nile, cut all water flowing to Egypt, force the closing of the Suez Canal, and thereby threaten England's vital link to India. Horrors! Based on this highly imaginative and very paranoid thinking, England began to build a railway from the port of Mombasa in Kenya to Uganda for the sole purpose of carrying English troops to Uganda to prevent the French from damming the Nile River and stopping any water from flowing to Egypt. It was an absolutely crazy plan, very difficult to build, and expensive. The railway had to be built from sea level up over 5,000-feet high across the dry, dusty plains of Kenya, across the Rift Valley, and then down to the tropical shores of Lake Victoria. Hundreds of men died from malnourishment, lions, and dysentery during its construction.

Note from the Future: Often, even crazy plans have positive aftereffects. When finished in 1901, the railway opened eastern Africa to development. Nairobi, today's capital of Kenya, grew from a small village to a modern metropolis due to the railway, and today the railway remains, one hundred years later, a major transportation link across eastern Africa.

- Quick Write: Stop for a moment and think of a crazy plan and how it might work. Write it down in a short paragraph and share it with the class when finished.
- Map Attack: On a blank map of the world, indicate all the features and how they all tie together in the crazy thinking behind the building of the Uganda Railway: India, the Suez Canal, Egypt, the Nile River, Uganda, Mombasa, Kenya, and the French.
- Poster Power: Create a job poster to recruit men to work on building the Uganda Railway at the turn of the century. Be sure to also mention the "crazy" reasons for building the railway and discount the "exaggerated" fears of workers being eaten by lions along the way.
- Front Page: In teams of four students each, create a front-page edition of the *Digital Times* on the building of the Uganda Railway. Include a map illustrating the reasons for building the railway and interviews with different people concerning the railway itself.

• Poet's Corner: Create a short epic poem or rap song describing the building of the Uganda Railway.
• You Were There: As the host of the popular TV program *You Were There*, have your studio audience write down three questions each to ask our guests today concerning the building of the Uganda Railway in 1901. Our guests (students in costume) for today are as follows:
  1. Bollregard Smedley—a British colonial officer responsible for the initial idea of the Uganda Railway.
  2. Lady Hildegarde Spoon—a member of the British royalty retired to Kenya. "Pip, Pip, and all that" was her favorite saying. She thought the builders of the railway were "bloody fools," to use Lady Spoon's exact words.
  3. Ravi Desai—a laborer recruited in India to work on the Uganda Railway who witnessed the immense hardship and suffering it took to build the railway that went nowhere.
  4. Bena Nakuru—a Kikuyu from Kenya who watched the railway being built past her village near Nairobi. She was amazed at how hard the British made everybody work on a project that seemed to make no sense.
• ADV Research: Using your library and the Internet, see if you can identify equally crazy plans by governments that were tremendously expensive and had little to show for their great expense.
• ADV Comparison: Using resources from your library and the Internet, compare the similarity of "domino" thinking that led to the building of the Uganda Railway to the thinking that led to the involvement of the United States in the fighting in Vietnam between 1965 and 1973.
• ADV Future Implications: The Ugandan Railway was a forewarning of the crazy paranoia of national rivalry of the early twentieth century in Europe. Using sources from the library and the Internet, trace the steps from the Uganda Railway incident onward that led to tragic opening of World War I.

7.3.2   Roosevelt's Canal Zone in Panama (1903)

The United States desperately wanted to build a canal across Central America to link its east coast with its west coast. The obvious choices were Nicaragua or Panama. A rich Frenchman by the name of Buneau-Varilla had already purchased a good deal of land in Panama for the purpose of building a canal—and obviously wanted to have the United

States build its canal in Panama. As a canal site for the United States, however, Panama had its problems. It was still part of Colombia, which had no desire to have a canal owned by the United States running through its country. Buneau-Varilla, however, had other ideas. On November 2, 1903, he and a few friends staged a small rebellion proclaiming Panama's independence from Colombia. As if by magic, a U.S. warship just happened to be nearby and was able to recognize the new Panamanian republic and to protect Buneau-Varilla from any Colombian counterattack. Without hesitation, the United States quickly signed the Hays Buneau-Varilla Treaty creating a United States Canal Zone in the two-week-old republic of Panama. When questioned whether such a canal was legal, President Roosevelt's Attorney General Philander Knox stated: "Oh, Mr. President do not let so great an achievement suffer from any taint of legality." The canal was finally opened in 1914.

- Quick Write: Write a short paragraph about a time when you saw somebody claim something as theirs when it really was not. What happened as a result of the incident?
- Pair Share: In pairs of two, have each partner discuss for one minute each the implications of the United States following international law and protocol or ignoring international law in its dealings with other nations.
- T Chart: Using a T Chart, compare each incident in the creation of the republic of Panama and the Canal Zone from the viewpoint of the United States on one side and from the viewpoint of the country of Colombia on the other side.
- Quick Skit: In a team of four, develop and present a short skit focused on the role Buneau-Varilla had in the establishment of the republic of Panama and the building of the Panama Canal.
- Art Mart: As a famed artist from 1903, create a drawing or painting that illustrates the way Buneau-Varilla and the United States staged their takeover of the area that would become Panama.
- ADV Comparison: Compare the way that the United States acquired the Canal Zone in Panama in 1903 with other international incidents, invasions, and assassinations throughout the twentieth century in which the United States was involved. Examples: Mossadeq in Iran (1953), Allende in Chile (1973), Grenada (1983), the Contras in Nicaragua (1982–1990), and Noriega in Panama (1989).

7.3.3   Moon Men (1969)

"We came in peace for all mankind" reads a plaque left on the moon in 1969 by the Apollo 11 crew. Great efforts such as those that place humans on the moon do not happen instantly. In 1961, President John Kennedy pledged to place a person on the moon by the end of the decade. Kennedy did not live long enough to see his pledge fulfilled, but as a nation, the United States kept this pledge and supported the Apollo lunar program of NASA (National Aeronautics and Space Administration) throughout the decade. The effort was not without its tragedy; one of the Apollo crews died instantly during a 1967 fire inside the module itself. After a careful resumption of the lunar program and four separate flights to the moon, Apollo 11 blasted off to the moon on July 21, 1969. Neil Armstrong and "Buzz" Alderin were the two lucky astronauts chosen to be the first humans to walk on the moon. Their first steps on the moon were tentative, but soon they were joyfully bounding around their lunar module at one-sixth the gravity of Earth, picking up rocks and taking photographs. In all they spent 21½ hours on the surface of the moon before they returned to their lunar command ship orbiting above. Much of the world cheered as they splashed down in the Pacific Ocean near Hawaii on July 26, 1969. The photographs of their leaping bounces across the moon are some of the most joyful of the twentieth century.

- Quick Write: In a short paragraph, describe the happiest moment of your life and share it with your classmates.
- Poster Power: Create a poster celebrating the first landing of Earthlings on the Moon.
- Moonling Message: Imagine yourself as an imaginary Moonling (invisible to most Earthlings) who witnesses the first landing of Earthlings on the Moon. Write a short description of what you saw and then share it with your fellow Moonlings (classmates).
- Front Page: In an editorial team of four student editors for the *Digital Times*, create a front-page edition celebrating the first landing on the moon by humans. Be sure to include interviews with astronauts (fellow students) and people who witnessed it on television, and include a map of the route taken by the astronauts.
- Quick Skit: With four team members, create a short skit demonstrating some of the drama of the first moon landing and include dialogue between the first astronauts on the moon and with Mission Control back on Earth.

- First Hand Sources: Have every student in class interview a parent, a neighbor, or a teacher who remembers what it was like when the astronauts first landed on the moon in 1969. Everyone should then write up their interview and share it with the class.
- ADV Futurist: Your team of four (students) has been hired by the United Nations to create a plan for a three-year trip to the planet Mars. You have one month to complete your mission and submit your plan to the full United Nations Assembly. Be sure to include your estimated costs, length of time, needed supplies, the route you plan to take to Mars, and the dates you recommend for the trip.

7.4.0 POLITICS AND LEADERSHIP

7.4.1 Gandhi—The Mahatma

Mohandas Gandhi (1869–1948)—the Mahatma (the Great Soul)—was truly one of the great political leaders of the twentieth century. His spirit has touched virtually every corner of our planet Earth. Gandhi was born in India but trained as a lawyer in England in 1889. He moved to South Africa in 1893 to practice law but was angered at the discrimination white South Africans showed to Indians living there. He began to practice nonviolent protests and civil disobedience to protest the mistreatment of his people. In 1905, after reading the ancient Indian epic poem *Bhagavad Gita*, Gandhi made the personal decision to abandon as many European ways of living as possible and return to the ways of ancient India. He chose celibacy as a way of life, abandoned all his worldly possessions, and wore only a loincloth and shawl. His protests were successful in South Africa; nondiscrimination laws were created to protect Indians living there. With a sense of triumph, he returned to his native India in 1915 with the goal of making India independent from England. World War I was raging in Europe and Gandhi supported the British during the war with the belief that such support would lead to independence. He was wrong. In 1919, near the end of the war, British troops attacked and killed hundreds of peaceful Indian protestors in the town of Amritsar. The killings at Amritsar sparked the beginning of the Indian nationalist movement and the move for Indian independence through nonviolent protests and civil disobedience. At the beginning of World War II, Gandhi volunteered to have India support the British war effort in return for independence. The English government re-fused and jailed Gandhi for most of the war. At the end of the war, however, the English government changed its mind, released Gandhi, and began to negotiate with him for Indian independence. The British, however, decided on their own that an independent India should be divided into a Muslim section (Pakistan) and a Hindu section (India). Gandhi was strongly against separating peoples on the basis of religion or caste, and opposed this division of India. In his nonviolent ways, he fought hard to keep all Indian peoples together in one united country. Just a few months before the independence of India and Pakistan, Gandhi was assassinated by a fanatical Hindu nationalist.

Notes from the Future: Gandhi, as the Hindu leader of the nonviolent Indian independence movement, got many of his ideas for nonviolence from the teaching of Jesus. Gandhi, in turn, became the model for the nonviolent protests during the Civil Rights movement led by Christian minister Dr. Martin Luther King in the United States during the 1960s.

- Quick Write: In a short paragraph, write a description of a time recently when you were angry at something you did not like. What did you do and what was the result of what you did?
- T Chart: Some new rules have been created in your community that you do not like. Compare violent and nonviolent ways of protesting these new rules and the advantages and disadvantages of each type of protest. As a result of your analysis, which method would you chose to oppose these new rules?
- Music Mart: Create a song or a rap telling the story of the Mahatma.
- Poster Power: Create a poster that illustrates the methods Gandhi used in his nonviolent protests for Indian independence.
- Quick Skit: With a team of four students, create a short skit illustrating the methods that Gandhi used to lead India to independence.
- Front Page: With a team of four student editors, create a front-page edition of the *Digital Times*, the leading cyber newspaper of the twentieth century, focusing on the nonviolent protest movement of Gandhi's independence movement.
- ADV Historical Research: Research your school library and the Internet to find examples of other nonviolent protests used at various times in history, such as the Civil Rights movement in the United States (1960s) and at Tienanmen Square in China (1989). What happened to these movement and why were they successful or not?

7.4.2   Churchill—Hero or Villain?

If there ever was an English patriot, it was Winston Churchill (1874–1965). From what we now know of history, Churchill was a major reason why the United States entered World War I (1914–1919) on the side of England. Was he a hero or a villain for this action? Let us take a closer look at what happened before we make a judgment. Two major events convinced the United States finally to enter the war on the side of England: the sinking of the steamship *Lusitania*—with hundreds of Americans on board—by a German submarine, and the Zimmerman telegram—intercepted by British intelligence—in which Germany tried to get Mexico to join the war against the United States.

How was Churchill connected to the *Lusitania* and the Zimmerman telegram? First, during the early part of the war, Churchill—as the head of the British war office—believed one of his major duties was to bring the United States into the war on the side of England. Very early, Britain broke the German secret radio codes and knew where the German submarines were located. Under Churchill's orders, the steamship *Lusitania,* with several hundred Americans on board, was deliberately not warned that it was sailing into an area of German submarines. As expected, German submarines torpedoed the *Lusitania.* Hundreds of Americans lost their lives and the *Lusitania* became a rallying cry for the Americans troops entering the war. Shortly after the *Lusitania* was torpedoed, an encrypted "Zimmerman telegram" from the German government to the Mexican government was intercepted by the British and transmitted to the United States. The telegram asked Mexico to fight with Germany against the United States. This telegram, along with the *Lusitania,* convinced the United States to enter the war. One problem: historians after the war found no evidence of the telegram being either sent or received in either Germany or Mexico. It is now believed that the telegram was a fake. We know it originally came from England, and likely from Churchill's office. Did he fake this telegram, as well as deliberately sinking the *Lusitania,* to get the United States to become an ally of England? Should we consider him a hero or a villain for such actions?

• Quick Write: Write a short paragraph on whether or not you think it is right for a person to do something wrong, like tell a lie for a good cause.

- Poster Power #1: Create a poster calling on the United States to enter World War I because of the *Lusitania* and the Zimmerman telegram.
- Poster Power #2: Create a poster calling on the United States *not* to enter World War I because of the false pretenses likely created by Churchill.
- Music Mart: Create a song or a rap questioning the entry of the United States into World War I.
- Front Page: With a team of four student editors, create a front-page edition of the *Digital Times*. Focus this edition on whether or not the United States should enter World War I due to the sinking of the *Lusitania* and the Zimmerman telegram.
- Counter Spin: As a representative of the German government in 1917, what would you say to the United States government concerning the *Lusitania* and the Zimmerman telegram in order to either discourage the United States from entering the war or have it support Germany in the war?
- Mock Trial: Stage a mock trial in your classroom with four students acting as the prosecuting attorneys and four acting as the defending attorneys and the rest of the class the jury. The question before the jury is whether Churchill should be judged a hero or a villain because of his actions in getting the United States into World War I.
- ADV Historical Research: Using your library and the Internet, try to find other instances in history where false evidence was used to make a major change in history.

7.4.3   Lenin and the Sealed Train to Helsinki (1917)

A mysterious sealed train left Switzerland in 1917. It crossed Germany secretly with all of its windows shuttered and no one was allowed to get on board. Some people saw a strange little bald man on board, but did not know who he was. The train was bound for Helsinki, Finland, and some men in German military uniforms took the little bald man to the Russian border and left him there. The little bald man was Lenin and the German soldiers on the train had orders from the high command of the German military to take him from where he was living in exile in Switzerland to the Russian border. Lenin was the leader of a group of Russian revolutionaries called the Bolsheviks and was kicked out of Russia for trying to overthrow the government of Russia. Germany in 1917 was in the middle of World War I fighting against England,

France, and Russia. To cause trouble for the Russian government of Tsar Nicholas II, Germany secretly shipped the Russian revolutionary —Lenin—back to Russia to cause trouble and disrupt the Russian war effort. Lenin was a firm believer in the teachings of Karl Marx and dreamed of making Russia into a "communist" state where all property and wealth would be held in common by the workers. The Germans did not believe in Marx, but just wanted Lenin to cause trouble in Russia. The German plan succeeded beyond their wildest imagination. The tsar's government was weak and so was the Russian army. Lenin's Bolsheviks and other revolutionaries just added to the chaos. Moderate social revolutionaries forced the tsar to step down in February 1917; by the end of the year, Lenin and the Bolsheviks were in control of large parts of a new Union of Soviet Socialist Republics (USSR). Under the communist Bolsheviks, Russia withdrew from the war, much to the irritation of its allies, England and the United States. The capitalist nations of England and the United States—supporting private ownership of large factories—strongly opposed "communist" control of a country as large as Russia.

Note from the Future: Although Lenin was an inspirational speaker and leader, the main force in creating the Soviet Union was a bank robber and treasurer of the Bolsheviks by the name of Joseph Stalin. His dictatorial rule unified the USSR into the major world power on a Marxist/Leninist model (opposed to the United States) during most of the twentieth century.

- Quick Write: In a short paragraph, describe a time when you wanted something very much and created a plan in order to get it. Did your plan work or not work? Describe why your plan succeeded or did not succeed.
- Map Attack: Using a blank map of Europe, illustrate the basic alliances of countries that fought each other during World War I: Germany, Austria, and Serbia on one side and England, France, Russia, and the United States on the other side. On the map, illustrate the impact the withdrawal of Russia from the war had on the war itself.
- You Were There: As the host of this popular TV program, have your studio audience (students in the class) write down questions concerning the Russian Revolution to ask the guests for this week's show:
  1. General Von Cutlow—the German general in charge of moving Lenin from Switzerland to Russia

2. Lenin—the Bolshevik leader of the Russian Revolution
3. Tsar Nicholas II—the aristocratic leader of Russia before the Revolution
4. Joseph Stalin—the man with the iron fist who forged the Soviet Union together after the death of Lenin

- Poster Power #1: Create a poster supporting Lenin and the Russian Revolution.
- Poster power #2: Create a poster opposing Lenin and the Russian Revolution.
- Quick Skit: With a team of four students, create a short skit of four Russians—a factory worker, a soldier, a peasant, and rich noble—illustrating the major problems that faced Russia in 1917.
- ADV Historical Research: Compare the Russian Revolution of 1917 with the American Revolution of 1776 and the French Revolution of 1789. How are they different and similar to each other? Report your findings to the class.

7.4.4   Adolf and the Nazis

Germany lost World War I to England, France, and the United States. The Treaty of Versailles unfairly blamed Germany for being the only cause of the war and forced Germany to pay England and France for their costs of the war. These "reparation" payments to England and France were a great burden on the German economy and almost automatically forced it into a depression after the war. The Germans were angry at what happened to them at Versailles. Quite often in such desperate times, people will begin to believe anyone as long as he gives them hope for better times. Such a man was a little Austrian racist by the name of Adolf Hitler. He had the answer, he said: "Ich bin der Führer!"—I am the leader.

The answer that Hitler gave was that the Jews were the cause of all the problems of the Germans. He blamed them for Germany's loss of the war. Of course it was not true, but like all good propaganda, he continued to repeat it often enough and most of the German people began to believe it. He also had an answer for pulling Germany out of the Great Depression: reject the Treaty of Versailles, stop paying reparations to England and France, and hire unemployed workers to rebuild Germany's military. Hitler's plan to end the Great Depression in Germany worked—millions of German workers were reemployed building bombers, tanks, and guns for Germany's military. But Hitler's simple answers for Germany's problems also had very predictable results: Hitler's racism resulted in the Nazi Holocaust and the murder of millions of Jews, gypsies, and other non-Germanic peoples. Hitler's military buildup also resulted in World War II. Together, these two events can be considered to be the major tragedies of the twentieth century.

- Quick Write: Think for a moment what would happen if you told your friends that this Friday had just been declared a national holiday and that there would be no school. How fast would your "untruth" spread across the campus? How many other students would believe it? What would likely happen at your school as a result of your "untruth"?
- Poster Power: Create a realistic Nazi poster from 1933 picturing Adolf Hitler screaming his slogan: "Ich bin der Führer!" (I am the leader).
- Counter Spin: Create a poster illustrating what happens to people who follow people like Hitler.
- Quick Skit: With a team of four actors (students), create a short skit that illustrates the ultimate tragedies of Hitler's simple solutions for the German people during the 1930s.
- Diary Entry: As a teenager in Nazi Germany, write in your diary what Hitler is doing to the country, the racism he is practicing, and his buildup of the German war machine.
- ADV Historical Research: Adolf Hitler is without question one of the most evil men in the history of the world. Use your library and the Internet to identify other evil men in history and compare them to Hitler. When completed, share your findings with your class.

7.4.5   Mao Ze-dong (1893–1976)

Few men have left their imprint on a country as strongly as Mao left his on China during the twentieth century. Mao was a communist follower of Marx and Lenin, but with a Chinese twist. Where Marx and Lenin insisted that the Russian communist revolution be focused on the urban factory workers, Mao worked to have the rural Chinese peasant be the center of his communist revolution.

At first, he was not very powerful because his followers constantly had to fight their bitter nationalist Chinese rival, Chiang Kai-shek. In an almost legendary trek, Mao and his followers traveled over 6,000 miles during their Long March of 1934–1935 to avoid being captured by Chiang's armies. The Japanese invasion of China during the 1930s

ironically gave Mao a chance to strengthen his military with the assistance of the Soviet Union. By 1949, Mao took control of China and
chased the nationalist followers of Chiang to the island of Taiwan. In
1958, Mao moved with his Great Leap Forward to form all of China
into his model of peasant revolutionaries. The Great Leap Forward
turned into one of the major tragedies of the twentieth century—an
estimated twenty million Chinese starved to death. In 1966, Mao tried
again to impose his revolutionary communist thought on the Chinese
people with the Cultural Revolution. Party youth marched across the
country waving Mao's Little Red Book of sayings and forcing workers to work in the fields as peasants. The Cultural Revolution died in
the early 1970s as Mao's power weakened. Mao died in 1976, but
Chairman Mao lives on as the major figure in Chinese history during
the twentieth century.

- Quick Write: What would you rather be: a factory worker or a peasant working in the fields? Write a short paragraph describing the reasons for your decision.
- Poster Power: Create a poster supporting Mao's peasant brand of
  communism.
- Counter Spin: Create a Russian Marxist/Leninist poster opposing
  Mao's form of rural peasant communism and supporting a revolution
  of factory workers.
- Front Page: With a team of four student editors, create a front-page
  edition of the *Digital Times*. Focus your special edition on Mao's radical form of peasant communism and the tragic failure of the Great
  Leap Forward in China in 1958.
- You Were There: As the host of this popular TV program, have your
  studio audience each write questions to ask our guests for the week
  concerning the influence of Mao Ze-dong on twentieth-century
  China. Our guests (students in costume) for the week will be:
  1. Ping Lee—Mao's chief secretary during the Cultural Revolution
  2. Dr. Zarkov—a strict Russian Marxist/Leninist opposed to Mao's
     form of communism
  3. Samuel Yee—an overseas Chinese millionaire, opposed to Mao, who
     looks forward to making China into a major capitalistic country
  4. Zi Chin—one of Mao's oldest followers who was with him on the
     Long March in 1935–1936
- ADV Historical Research: Do further reading on the tragic failure of
  Mao's Great Leap Forward in 1958 in your school library and on the

Internet. As a result of your readings, do you think that Mao should be viewed as a historical villain who killed twenty million people, or as a tragic hero of the Chinese people who really had the good of his people in his heart and should be forgiven for accidentally causing the death of twenty million people?

7.4.6   The Cold War—A Warlike Un-War (1945–1990)

For forty-five years (1945–1990), an intense ideological "Cold War" between Russia (the USSR) and the United States dominated almost every facet of the era's world politics and threatened several times to break into a full-scale war of mutual destruction. Even today, it is a matter of ideological debate as to who started the Cold War and even how it ended. In reality, the two systems of governing are opposites: the capitalist system of the United States has rich individuals controlling the economy of the nation while the socialist system of Russia has the state government controlling the economy. Before World War II, the two systems of government were opposed to each other, and after World War II, they were again locking horns with each other.

- History Chain #1: Below is a brief, randomized chronology of the Cold War. Make large 8-½"-x-11" historical event cards for each of the twenty-three historical events below. Give one historical event card to each student, and have each hold the card in front of him or her so all the other students can see it. When finished, have all twenty-three students rearrange themselves chronologically across the room— oldest year to the most recent year. Reorder it in chronological order and follow the activities below to begin to make sense of these phenomena that dominated much of the last half of the twentieth century:
  1. Cuban Missile Crisis (1962): U.S. President Kennedy threatened war when Russia set up missiles in Cuba, but compromised by agreeing to have the United States withdraw missiles from Turkey in exchange for Russia's withdrawing missiles from Cuba.
  2. Gorbachev (1985): USSR President Gorbachev attempted to revive a long-declining Soviet economy by opening many sectors of the economy, freeing political expression, and ending the Cold War through peaceful negotiations.
  3. NATO (1949): The United States and its allies formed a European military alliance against Russia.

4. Sputnik (1957): The Russians put the first artificial satellite into orbit around the Earth, escalating the Cold War into a "race for space."

5. Korea (1950): North Korea invaded South Korea and threatened to escalate the Cold War into a full nuclear war.

6. Iron Curtain (1946): Churchill gave a speech in Fulton, Missouri, in which he described an "iron curtain" of communism descending across Eastern Europe.

7. Evil Empire (1981): U.S. President Reagan revived the intensity of the Cold War by calling the USSR (Russia) an "evil empire" and rapidly increasing U.S. military expenditures.

8. H-Bomb (1952): The United States detonated the first hydrogen bomb, greatly increasing the destructive capability of any future war.

9. Greece (1947): To prevent a "communist" take over of Greece, the United States provided military aid to a dictatorship ruling Greece and called it a "bastion of liberty." It was the first of a large number of such dictatorships across the world that the United States would support during the Cold War in the name of "stopping communism."

10. Death of Stalin (1953): The death of the dictator Stalin in Russia changed the leadership in the Soviet Union, but did little to ease the Cold War.

11. Berlin Airlift (1948): After the Soviet blockade of Berlin, Germany, the United States flew in supplies around the clock to keep Berlin supplied with food and coal for the winter.

12. Berlin Wall Comes Down (1989): As a sign of Gorbachev's loosening of the USSR's control of Eastern Europe, the Berlin Wall is taken down.

13. Red China (1949): Mao Ze-dong took control of Mainland China, creating the People's Republic of China.

14. End of the USSR (1991): In 1991, unable to revive the economy and faced with widening ethnic tensions across the USSR, the USSR was officially dissolved in favor of the separate states of Russia and the other former Soviet republics. The Cold War was now officially over.

15. Marshall Plan (1947): To prevent Western European countries from "falling to the communists," the United States provided large amounts of aid to the countries of Western Europe, such as Germany, France, and Italy, to rebuild their countries after World War II.

16. Massive Retaliation (1958): Under President Eisenhower and his Secretary of State Dulles, the Cold War heated up again when the United States announced a program of "massive retaliation" to stop Russian expansion. The result was a rapid build-up of nuclear weapons and a threat of nuclear devastation.

17. Anti-American Campaign (1947): Responding to the Truman Doctrine, Stalin revived his anti-American propaganda campaign and worldwide efforts to spread socialism.

18. Berlin Wall (1961): In a show of brute strength, but a sign of weakness, Russia constructed a cement wall around Berlin to prevent Eastern Germans from escaping to the West.

19. Hiroshima (1945): The United States dropped the atomic bomb on Hiroshima, Japan, to speed up the end of the war, and also to intimidate the Russians who were set to invade Japan from the north.

20. Afghanistan (1979–1989): The USSR trapped itself in Afghanistan in a prolonged ground war attempting to support a pro-Russian government, but failed.

21. Truman Doctrine (1947): President Truman declared that the goal of the United States was to "contain" and "root out" communism wherever it appeared in the world. This became the goal of the United States for the next forty years during the Cold War.

22. Eastern Europe (1946): Russia set up socialist governments in the countries it conquered in Eastern Europe.

23. Vietnam (1961–1973): The United States trapped itself into a prolonged ground war in Vietnam in the belief that it must "contain" communism.

- History Chain #2: Once the history chain is in chronological order across the room, have the class identify which historical items are the possible causes of the Cold War and then determine who was the major cause—the USSR or the United States.

- History Chain #3: Looking at the history chain in front of the class, have the class identify the events in the Cold War that threatened to escalate into a full nuclear war between the USSR and the United States. What are the possible reasons why a full nuclear war did not develop between the USSR and the United States?

- History Chain #4: Looking at the history chain in front of the class, look at possible periods when the Cold War could have ended. What reasons can be given for the reescalation of it?

- History Chain #5: Looking at the history chain in front of the class, what causes can we attribute to the ending of the Cold War? Was the United States or the USSR more responsible for ending the Cold

War? (Note: This is the end of the history chain activity. The teacher may collect the twenty-three "Cold War Historical Event Cards" to use them again at a later date.)

- ADV What If?: In teams of four, students can hypothesize what would have happened if the Cold War had never taken place between the USSR and the United States.
  1. Would the lack of competition between the two countries have resulted in slow growth and very few new innovations, such as computers and rockets to the moon?
  2. Or would a peaceful competition between the two countries have resulted in a much more nonmilitaristic programs for the poorer countries of the world, a stronger United Nations, and an established UN Mars colony already in existence?

7.5.0   SOCIAL AND ECONOMIC LIFE

7.5.1   The Twentieth-Century Middle Class

One of the most powerful phenomena of the twentieth century was the middle class of modern nation-states. During the late eighteenth century, the middle class was the major participant in the French Revolution, overthrowing the power of the nobility above them. During the nineteenth century, this newly empowered class of people became more conservative as they worked hard to hold onto the financial gains they made. In direct contradiction to these rights "for all the people" so nobly proclaimed in both the American and French Revolutions, the middle class often fought long and hard to prevent the lower working classes from achieving any political economic or social rights. They also believed passionately in their own nation-states and the mythology that was created around these states. They believed strongly that their own nation was superior to other nations. They were willing to go to war for the "honor" of their nation-state over very minor and questionable incidents. They were also willing to be taxed at very heavy rates to finance these wars for national "glory."

Under a king, a country went to war when the king decided to fight. How does a nation ruled by a middle class decide to go to war? The middle-class nation must be convinced that the war is good for their country or protecting their country's interests. A propaganda blitz by the national media of the United States against Spain and popular music lyrics such as "I wanna go to war . . ." from Alexander's Ragtime Band before the Spanish American War successfully convinced the American middle class that war with Spain was necessary. Even as recently as the Vietnam War, a questionable event of U.S. ships being attacked was used by the President and mass media to successfully win middle-class support for sending more U.S. troops to Vietnam (see TLP 7.7.6 Gulf of Tonkin—1964; Ulich 1971, 13–14).

- Quick Write: In a short paragraph, give a description of the middle class in your town. What do they look like? Where do they live? What kind of jobs do they have? What kind of political beliefs do they have? What do they do for fun?
- Action Research: To test personal impressions of the middle class in the Quick Write above, conduct a survey—done by members of the class—to ask the same questions to the neighbors of each student:
  1. What do they look like?
  2. Where do they live?
  3. What kind of jobs do they have?
  4. What kind of political beliefs do they have?
  5. What do they do for fun?
  Note: When finished, compare the initial impressions of the class in the quick writes with the results of the action research completed by the students of the class.

- Poster Power: Design a propaganda (advertising) poster to convince the middle class of the United States to go to war with another country.
- Counter Spin: Design a propaganda (advertising) poster to convince the middle class of the United States to oppose going to war with another country.
- Front Page: In teams of four student editors, create a front-page edition of the *Digital Times* on the impact of the middle class on the politics of the century across the world. Be sure to conduct interviews of potential members of the "middle class" among the members of the classroom and illustrate what they will look like in the future.
- ADV Research Project: Using your school library and the Internet, explore alternatives to the modern nation-states. Can the people of the world live in other types of political organizations—such as a United Federation of Nations—during the twenty-first century?

7.5.2   The Great Depression: The Causes (1929)

In October 1929, the stock market crashed on Wall Street in New York City. It was the beginning of the Great Depression (1929–1939), which caused untold suffering across the world. As a result of the crash of 1929, banks closed because they had no more money, companies closed and laid off their employees because people were no longer buying things, and many people starved because they did not have enough to eat. The prosperity that the capitalist financial system promised to the world during the 1920s came down with a grinding crash. The depression was also a contributing cause of the Second World War because Adolf Hitler was able to come to power due to the tragic effects of the Great Depression in Germany.

What caused the Great Depression? The economists tell us that too many banks were lending money to people to put into risky companies. When these risky companies failed, the investors lost their money and so did the banks. Other people in turn panicked and lost faith in the whole monetary system from the stock market to their own banks and withdrew their money from both. The Great Depression could have been stopped, or at least slowed down, but the leaders of the world either did nothing, or did the wrong things to fight it. President Hoover, the president of the United States during the actual crash of 1929, did nothing, believing that the economy would naturally right itself. He might have been correct but, in 1931, the United States Congress decided that American jobs needed to be protected from foreign competition and passed the Smoot-Hawley Bill that raised high tariffs (taxes) on all imports from foreign counties. In effect, the Smoot-Hawley cut off all foreign trade with other countries; as a result, other countries ceased to purchase things from the United States. Instead of increasing employment, the Smoot-Hawley Bill decreased the number of jobs in the country and in the world as a whole because companies could no longer make things for export overseas. The world sank deeper into the Great Depression as a result of this ill-advised law by the United States Congress.

- Quick Write: What if your parents lost their jobs and you had no relatives to care for you? Write a short paragraph describing what you would do in this situation and share your thoughts with the class.
- Art Mart: On a large piece of paper, illustrate the suffering the Great Depression caused people across the world.
- Poet Power: Create a poem or a rap that illustrates the hardship people had to endure during the Great Depression.

- Graffiti: On a large piece of paper, create a strongly worded wall graffiti that is openly critical of the world leaders who did nothing or the wrong thing to end the Great Depression.
- Front Page: With a team of four student editors, create a front-page edition of the *Digital Times* focusing on the 1929 stock market crash and the Great Depression that followed shortly afterward. Be sure to interview people who suffered during the crash and political leaders who did not do a very good job of stopping the Great Depression.
- ADV Historical Research: Using your school library and the Internet, identify other economic depressions in recent world history and compare the suffering they caused people compared to the Great Depression of 1929–1939.

7.5.3   Attacking the Great Depression (1933)

In 1933—deep into the Great World Depression—three different and successful means were used to slowly bring the Great Depression to an end. President Franklin Roosevelt of the United States in 1933 attacked the depression through his New Deal "bully pulpit" and continually told the American people in his fireside radio chats that "the only thing you have to fear is fear itself." He backed this up with an active governmental program of creating liquidity in the economy by making sure banks had enough money, making loans available for people to buy more things, creating more jobs through government projects such as building dams and highways, reopening foreign trade by lowering tariffs, and generally restoring the people's faith in the economy. The second major approach to combat the depression was with a socialist economy such as existed in the Soviet Union during most of the twentieth century. The Soviet Union did not experience the depression because the government controlled the economy, set all the prices, and was excluded from the rest of the world economy by the other capitalist countries who opposed the socialist type of government and economy. The Russian people did not become rich under the Soviet system during the Great Depression, but everybody was working. In Germany, Adolf Hitler and the Nazis attacked the depression a third way—by military expenditure. Hitler rebuilt the German economy during the 1930s by employing millions of German workers to build new tanks, guns, uniforms, and airplanes. Hitler's efforts worked. They stimulated the German economy and created a prosperous German economy during the late 1930s. Unfortunately, Hitler did not stop there; instead, he led the world down the path to World War II with his large new military.

- Quick Write: Imagine you are homeless and living out in the street. Write a short paragraph describing jobs you could create to earn enough money to live on and pull yourself out of being homeless. When finished, share your thoughts with the class.
- Double T Chart: Using a double T chart (with three columns), compare the three successful means of combating the Great Depression — Roosevelt's New Deal, the USSR's controlled socialist economy, and the Nazi's military machine. From your analysis, which one do you think is the best and which is the worst? Give your reasons to support your thinking.
- Poster Power: Create a large poster advertising one of the three ways to combat the Great Depression — the American way, the Soviet way, or the German way.
- You Were There: As the host of this popular TV program, have each member of your studio audience (the class) write three questions for our very important guests (students in costume) this week who will present their views on how to combat the Great Depression. Our distinguished guests from the past are as follows:
  1. Franklin Roosevelt — president of the United States during the Great Depression
  2. Joseph Stalin — premiere of the Soviet Union during the Great Depression
  3. Adolf Hitler — leader of Germany during the Great Depression
- ADV Historical Analysis: Using resources in your school library and on the Internet, compare the three methods of combating the Great Depression with current methods the United States and other countries use to prevent another Great Depression from happening.
- ADV Planning for the Future: Make a list of useful, peaceful governmental projects that can be used to stimulate the economy by employing many people in the future when an economic depression or recession is threatening (for example, space exploration).

7.6.0 RELIGIOUS THOUGHT

7.6.1   The Protestant Ethic (1920)

Max Weber (1864–1920) wrote *The Protestant Ethic and Capitalism* (1920), in which he describes what motivates humans to work hard and earn more money. He disagreed with other economists such as Karl Marx who believed that humans were motivated only by economic need. Weber believed that humans had other forces to guide them—a motivational leader, an inspirational song, or most importantly, a strong religious belief concerning work. He was curious why capitalism—the creation of wealth through private ownership—worked well in some countries but not in others. In his study, he found that capitalism was most successful in countries such as the United States that were dominated by Protestant Christian churches. Protestants, he found, were motivated to work hard because they believed that if they were to be "saved" by their own God, it would be by their own "faith supported by good works." Catholics, Weber found, believed they could be "saved" by having their local priest forgive all their sins. Catholics, according to Weber, were not as good capitalists as Protestants because the Protestants were driven to work hard by their religion.

- Quick Write: Personally, what makes you work hard—the knowledge that you are going to earn money, that you like to work, or your religious beliefs? Write a short paragraph describing what you think about this subject and share it with your class.
- Viewpoints: Four distinguished panel members (students in class) are here to discuss the issue of the Protestant work ethic and capitalism. Every member of the audience should have a question to ask them. The panel members are as follows:
  1. Enrique Delgado—Father Delgado is a Spanish Catholic priest who believes that it is wrong for Christians to be capitalists and to want to earn money. A good Christian says Delgado will give his money to the poor and to the Church.
  2. Samuel Carnegie—Mr. Carnegie is a wealthy capitalist and owner of a chain of important banks. He believes that his capitalist beliefs have nothing to do with religion.
  3. Emil Smith—Mr. Smith is a good, hard-working carpenter and churchgoer—to a Protestant church. He believes that his religious beliefs and his hard work as a carpenter go together.
  4. Suzie Davenport—Ms. Davenport is a practicing Buddhist who runs her own successful accounting company. She does not think her religion has anything to do with her success as a businesswoman. She likes, however, how Buddhism relaxes her and clears her mind to make important decisions.
- Action Research: Each student in class should ask parents, friends, and neighbors whether they think that their religion is connected to their concept of earning money and hard work.

• Plenary Session: When finished with their action research, the class should convene a plenary session to discuss whether or not they have found Max Weber's thesis linking capitalism to Protestantism to be true or not.

7.7.0   CONQUEST AND WARFARE

7.7.1   Who Caused World War I?

The tale is told of the scorpion and the frog—where the frog agrees to carry the scorpion across a stream of water if the scorpion promises not to sting and kill the frog. The scorpion, however, stings the frog in the middle of the stream. The frog, in his dying breath, asks the scorpion why he stung him. The scorpion answers that he did it because he was a scorpion and scorpions sting and kill frogs. As a result, both the scorpion and the frog died. The tale is a metaphor of World War I where the leaders of Europe were all willing to go to war as a matter of pride and honor for their own nations—regardless of the human and economic costs. In reality, World War I was the last war of the nineteenth century where war between nations was honorable and noble. The new weapons of the twentieth century made such "honorable and noble" notions of warfare obsolete, if not suicidal.

Six European nations were at the center of World War I:

1. Serbia—The Serbs were proud of their little nation and wanted to be treated like a major European power. To show their national pride, they sought to liberate fellow Serbs in neighboring Austria-Hungary. A Serb fanatic assassinated the Archduke Ferdinand of Austria-Hungary on June 28, 1914, starting the chain reaction that resulted in World War I.
2. Russia—Russia wanted to prove that it was an important European nation with a large army like other European nations. As part of its pride to build its national spirit, Russia fanned pro-Slavic nationalism (the Serbs are Slavs) and supported the actions of Serbia.
3. Austria-Hungary—The large old Austro-Hungarian Empire was threatening to fall apart. The rulers in Vienna were more interested in their former glory than the needs of the people. As a result, many of the ethnic groups within the empire, such as the Serbs, fought to break away and form their own states. In 1912 and 1913—immediately be-

fore World War I—the old empire fought to control the rebellious ethnic groups in Bosnia-Herzegovina in the Balkans.

4. Germany—Newly unified Germany wanted to exert its new national pride with new colonies and territory. Germany was also willing to strongly support neighboring Austria-Hungary in its problems with the Serbs.

5. France—France lost the Franco-Prussian War with Germany in 1870–1871 and thought of nothing more than revenge in order to satisfy its national pride against neighboring Germany.

6. England—Great Britain had the largest empire in the world in 1914 and wanted to do anything to protect it and perhaps increase it. Throughout the early twentieth century, Germany was the aggressor in seeking new colonies around the world and threatened the British empire on almost every continent. England would like to have the chance to lessen Germany's threat of further overseas expansion.

Historical Note #1: The winners of World War I—France, England, and a reluctant United States—blamed Germany for causing the war and forced it to pay reparations to France and England after the war. The question, however, remains if Germany really was the cause of World War I.

Historical Note #2: Two hundred fifty thousand Africans died during World War I with the promise that they would be granted freedom after the war. The promise never materialized until after World War II.

- Quick Write: In a short paragraph, describe why it is both good and bad to have pride in your country (nation). When finished, give examples of when this pride can become too great.
- Map Attack: On a blank map of Europe, name and illustrate the major European countries involved in World War I.
- They Did It!: Six students are to stand in front of the room. Each has a sign in front of them identifying which of the six countries (above) they represent. The teacher will ask each country (student) in turn: "Who started World War I?" Each country, in turn, will point their finger at the neighboring country and answer in turn as follows:
  1. Serbia will answer that Austria-Hungary started the war (and then list the reasons why this country is at fault).
  2. Austria-Hungary will answer that England started the war (and then list the reasons why this country is at fault).

3. England will answer that Russia started the war (and then list the reasons why this country is at fault).
4. Russia will answer that France started the war (and then list the reasons why this country is at fault).
5. France will answer that Germany started the war (and then list the reasons why this country is at fault).

- Poster Power: Students representing one of the six countries listed above should design a poster illustrating who they think caused World War I from the viewpoint of that country—and, of course, their own country was not at fault.
- Quick Skit: In student teams of four, each team should represent one of the six European nations above who was involved in the start of World War I. Each team can then develop a short skit that illustrates the extreme nationalism of the period, the intense rivalry between these nations of Europe, and the viewpoint of that nation as to who caused World War I.
- ADV Plenary Session: Students representing each of the above European nations should sit in a general plenary session and devise a plan by which World War I could have been avoided.

7.7.2 Japan's Hundred Years War

Between 1853 (Perry's forcible opening of Japan) and 1945 (Japan's defeat in World War II), Japan continually fought the United States and Europe to restore its independence and to retain its honor. From this viewpoint, Japan's warfare during the early twentieth century— including its war with Russia in 1905 and its attack against a European-dominated China during the 1930s—all led to an independence of Asia from Europe during the second half of the twentieth century. The Russo-Japanese War of 1905 was the first war that demonstrated an Asian country could defeat a European power. Japan's attack against China after 1937 created the negative chaos that weakened European control over China and enabled Mao and communism to come to power and destroy all aspects of European colonialism in China. The weak independence Japan gave former European colonies in Asia during World War II also allowed Asian countries their first step toward a real move for independence. In the standard American world history textbook, Japan quickly became industrialized throughout the twentieth century; with its new, modern army, Japan sought to conquer and control much of Asia. From this Japanese viewpoint, Japan was the crucial force that created the initial conditions from which Asian honor was restored and independence from Europe was achieved after World War II (Palmer 1974, 152–153).

- Quick Write: In a short paragraph, describe a recent incident you recall in which several people you know had very different memories and interpretations of what happened in the incident. What was the result of this difference of interpretation?
- Time Line: Create a time line of the major events (described above) of Japanese history between the opening of Japan in 1853 to the end of World War II in 1945.
- Venn Diagram: Using a regular world history textbook and the paragraph above, compare the differences between the regular American interpretation of Japanese history and the Japanese version of the same history on both sides of the diagram. In the middle, place the items on which they agree.
- Poster Power #1: Create a poster that illustrates the Japanese version of the history of Japan after 1853.
- Poster Power #2: Create a poster that illustrates the American version of the history of Japan after 1853.
- Quick Skit: In a team of four students, create a skit in which four scholars are arguing about whether the Japanese or the American view of recent Japanese history is correct.
- ADV Historical Research: Using your school library or the Internet, find at least one other incident in history where there are very different interpretations of what happened in history.

7.7.3   World War II—Could It Have Been Stopped?

World War II could have been stopped at any number of points, but it was not:

1. The Great Depression (1929–1939) caused untold suffering, desperation, and anger among many people around the world. The governments of the world, however, did nothing or often the wrong things, such as blocking foreign trade, resulting in people willing to listen to men with extreme solutions.
2. Totalitarian dictatorships arose in Germany, Italy, and Japan when desperate men began to follow extreme leaders during the Great Depression. The other countries of the world, such as the United States

and England, did little or nothing to stop the rise of these militaristic dictators. They were still exhausted from World War I and had little interest in stopping potential troublemakers in the world.
3. The capitalistic leaders of the United States and England during the Great Depression saw their major threat as communist Russia. As a result, they tolerated and even supported the dictators in Germany, Italy, and Japan because they were "anti-communist."

The United States refused to support the League of Nations after World War I and therefore did not give the League enough power to stop the aggression of these three nations before World War II. As a result, the three dictatorships saw the rest of the world as weak and continued their aggression.

The Versailles Treaty that ended World War I treated Germany unfairly, blaming it solely for the cause of the war and making it pay reparations costs to France and England. This unfair treatment caused a great deal of resentment and anger in Germany that in turn resulted in the aggressive militaristic actions of Germany during the 1930s.

- Quick Write: In a short paragraph, describe your ideas about whether you should attack a small problem before it becomes big, or wait until it becomes a big problem and then attack it. When finished, share your ideas with the class. (This was the major question during the 1930s before World War II—unfortunately, the world waited until it became a big problem.)
- Bumper Sticker: Create a bumper sticker for everybody's Model T Ford that calls for dealing with Hitler, Mussolini, and the Japanese *now* (in the 1930s) rather than waiting for World War II to start.
- Poster Power: Create a poster that illustrates one of the five major problems the world faced during the 1930s but did not deal with before the start of the war.
- Quick Skit: Teams of four students can create short skits that illustrate one of the five above world problems that led to World War II.
- Attack It Now!: In teams of four League of Nations representatives (students), each team should take one of the five "small" problems (1–5 above) that faced the world during the 1930s, and devise a plan to attack and solve the problem now rather than wait for the problem to increase in size and become a cause of the coming World War II. When finished, teams can share their solutions with the League of Nations (class).

- ADV Historical Research: Using your library and the Internet, look back in history for turning points where immediate action could have prevented a war.
- ADV The Futurist: Look at current newspapers, magazines, and the Internet to discover potential major world problems that need solving today, before they become out of control (for example: global warming). When finished, share your findings with the class.

7.7.4   Stalingrad (September 1942 to February 1943)—The Winter

In a short four months, in a single large Russian city—Stalingrad (the modern city of Volgograd), in a bitterly cold winter, two million Russian and German soldiers died during World War II. Just as Moscow was the turning point in Napoleon's war against Russia over one hundred years earlier, Stalingrad was the turning point in Germany's war against Russia during World War II. Hitler, after his conquest of most of Europe (1939–1941), ordered that Germany's gigantic army attack the Soviet Union (Russia) in Operation Barbarossa. It was late spring (June 1941) and Hitler was confident that his army could easily conquer its large neighbor to the east. The attack was careful planned—his troops went to war with plenty of airplanes, tanks, and troops, but Hitler did not add one thing into his plans: the Russian winter. Hitler sent his troops into Russia without any winter clothing. He was confident that this army could conquer Russia before winter started. When the fury of the Russian winter hit, the German army was not prepared. The generals of his army asked Hitler to pull back and camp for the winter; he refused and told his army to continue its attack. Hundreds of thousands of German soldiers froze to death at Stalingrad. The bitter winter was a major factor in Germany's loss of the Battle of Stalingrad and eventually all of World War II (Zentner 1963).

- Cold Write: In a short paragraph, describe the coldest you have ever been. What happened?
- Art Mart: In a sketch or painting, illustrate two armies trying to fight in a howling Russian winter at forty degrees below zero, when movement and even breathing is difficult.
- Map Attack: On a blank map of the world, locate Stalingrad in Russia; with an arrow indicate the route of the German army's attack across Russia during World War II and where they were stopped at Stalingrad in late 1942.

- Poster Power #1: Create a poster from the Russian point of view that celebrates the Soviet victory at Stalingrad.
- Poster Power #2: Create a poster that illustrates the German point of view and mourns the huge German losses at Stalingrad during World War II.
- Front Page: With a team of four student editors, create a front-page edition of the *Digital Times* newspaper describing the massive battle of Stalingrad that was the turning point of World War II. Be sure to include interviews with soldiers who fought on both sides, a map of where the conflict took place, and a description of the fierce Russian winter.
- ADV Historical Research: Using your school library and the Internet, compare Napoleon's failed invasion of Russia with Hitler's failed invasion of Russia during World War II.

7.7.5   Stalingrad (September 1942 to February 1943)—Racism

Racism was one of the major beliefs of Hitler and his Nazi Party. They blamed the Jews for Germany's loss of World War I and they saw the German people as superior to all other people, including their Slavic neighbors to the east in Russia. The Nazis believed the Russians would be easy to conquer because they thought that Germans were superior to the Slavic Russians. The Germans made very careful plans in their Operation Barbarossa and one thing they did not calculate was the large number of Russians and other Slavs who were willing to fight with the Nazis against the army of the Joseph Stalin and the Soviet Union. Stalin had ruled the Soviet Union during the 1930s with an iron fist, and million of Russians and other Slavs in the Soviet Union saw the Germans as liberators against Stalin's rule. The Germans during the first few months of the war captured millions of Russian soldiers and generals, and many were willing to change sides to fight for the Germans against Stalin. Hitler and the Nazis refused the offer of assistance of these "inferior" people. They believed they could fight the war with only German soldiers but they were wrong. The Germans lost the Battle of Stalingrad and began to retreat slowly back toward Germany. The battle was the turning point of World War II—the USSR and its allies, the United States and England, were now beginning to win the war. Without the racism of the Nazis, but with several million more Russian soldiers fighting for Hitler, the Battle of

Stalingrad and the result of World War II might have been very different (Zentner 1963).

- Quick Write: In a short paragraph, describe an incident in your life when someone acted against another person because of who they were or their ethnicity. What happened as a result of this incident? If you had been in control of the incident, how would you have handled it?
- Quick Skit: In a team of four students, create a short skit that illustrates two Russian soldiers who are willing to fight for Hitler against Stalin and the Russian Army trying to convince two German soldiers who do not want to let them fight on their side.
- T Chart: Using a T chart, compare the rationale of the Germans on one side for not using the Russian volunteers during the war and the rationale of the Russians who are willing to fight for the Germans against Stalin. In your view, which is the better argument?
- Bumper Sticker: Create a bumper sticker for the backside of a German tank that calls for the Germans to use Russian soldiers during World War II.
- ADV What If?: Using the library and the Internet as resources, research and then speculate on what might have happened if Hitler had accepted one to two million Russian soldiers into his army. Would that have been enough for Hitler to defeat the Russians at Stalingrad and prolong World War II? Would it have been enough for Hitler to win World War II?
- ADV Time Traveler: In teams of four, create an advertising plan for the future to combat racism and to treat everyone fairly.

7.7.6   Gulf of Tonkin (1964)

On August 6, 1964, the headlines of the highly respected *Washington Post* screamed "American Planes Hit North Vietnam after Second Attack on Our Destroyers: Move Taken to Halt New Aggression." Two days later, U.S. President Lyndon Johnson announced that due to the attacks on U.S. ships by North Vietnam in the Gulf of Tonkin, the United States would not spare any expense to protect the lives of its servicemen from unprovoked attacks and would commit large numbers of American troops to South Vietnam to protect the lives of our allies there. President Johnson announced retaliatory bombing against North Vietnam and asked the U.S. Senate to give him authority to intervene in Vietnam to protect the American boys stationed there and to prevent South Vietnam from falling to the communists. The U.S. Senate followed President Johnson's request. It was the formal beginning to America's tragic direct military involvement in Vietnam.

But let us take a closer look at the Gulf of Tonkin incident in 1964:

1. The year 1964 was a presidential election year pitting conservative Republican Barry Goldwater against moderate Democrat incumbent Lyndon Johnson. Goldwater had successfully been winning votes by attacking Johnson as being "soft on communism," especially in places such as Vietnam.
2. Johnson wanted to win the election but not appear to be the aggressor against North Vietnam. He wanted to counter Goldwater's charge about being "weak."
3. Johnson, as a person, did not like criticism and slowly rejected many of his advisors—even his vice president and the military joint chiefs of staff. He now made many major decisions by consulting only with his secretary of defense, Robert McNamara.
4. The United States had been secretly attacking North Vietnam for some time before August 1964.
5. In August 1964, two U.S. destroyers—the Maddox and the Turner Joy—had been shelling the Vietnamese coastline during the day. Two small North Vietnamese torpedo boats may have or may not have fired at the two much larger U.S. destroyers in response to the shelling—we do not know for sure.
6. Whether or not the small torpedo boats fired on the much larger U.S. ships, naval officers of the U.S. destroyers reported the incident to Washington. Military sources in Washington, in turn, reported the incident to the U.S. newspapers saying that U.S. ships had been attacked—but did not mention the previous attacks by the two U.S. ships on North Vietnam.
7. The U.S. newspapers, in turn, exaggerated what was told to them, resulting in headlines such as the one in the *Washington Post*.
8. U.S. President Lyndon Johnson—acting very much alone, without many advisors and with the upcoming election on his mind—asked for and received the support of the U.S. Senate to directly involve the military of the United States in the war in Vietnam. The Vietnamese had been fighting for independence since 1945. The United States was entering the war to "stop communist aggression." It was to be a tragic decision (McMaster 1997).

- Quick Write #1: In a short paragraph, describe an incident in your life when you exaggerated something. What happened as a result of your exaggeration?
- Quick Write #2: In a short paragraph, describe an incident in your life when you made a foolish decision without consulting anyone on what you really should have done.
- Map Attack: On a blank map of Asia, locate the Gulf of Tonkin next to Vietnam and draw a picture of two U.S. naval destroyers in the gulf. Add two small North Vietnamese torpedo boats in a picture with a question mark beside them to indicate our uncertainty as to what happened that day in 1964.
- Quick Skit: With four students, create a short skit that illustrates how the news of the possible "attack" on the U.S. ships spread and "accidentally" became exaggerated from the ships themselves, to the military in Washington, and finally to the newspapers.
- Counter Spin: In another team of four students, argue that the exaggeration of the attack was *not* accidental but deliberate, to create support in the United States for retaliation against the North Vietnamese and to provide a rationale for a president—wanting to win an election—to have a valid excuse to ask the Senate for support to enlarge the war in Vietnam.
- Front Page: In an editorial team of four students, create a front-page edition of the *Digital Times* newspaper that reports the Gulf of Tonkin incident with gigantic headlines, scare tactics, and exaggerations of what happened.
- Counter Front Page: In a second editorial team of four students, create a front-page edition of the paper reporting the incident very carefully and as factually as possible with interviews, maps, and editorials.
- Action Research: Each student should examine a local newspaper at home to determine how often the paper reports things carefully and accurately or how often the paper uses gigantic headlines, scare tactics, and exaggerations of news events.
- ADV Historical Research #1: Using the library and the Internet as sources, go back to old newspapers before any war or conflict to see how often newspapers in the past resorted to exaggerations to possibly influence public opinion in favor of the war.
- ADV Historical Research #2: Using the library and the Internet, look for other instances in history when political leaders have created wars to boost their political popularity.

7.8.0 TRAGEDY AND DISASTER

7.8.1 The Nazi Holocaust

In one of the most tragic acts of inhumanity in history, an estimated six million Jewish men, women, and children were systematically killed by the Nazis during the Holocaust (1941–1945). In the same process, thousands of gypsies, handicapped individuals, mentally ill persons, homosexuals, and sympathetic Germans were also killed by the Nazis during the Holocaust. Christian Europe had a long history of anti-Jewish violence, starting during the Middle Ages and stemming from a twisted belief that blamed the death of Jesus on the Jews, not the Romans. Adolf Hitler played on this anti-Jewish sentiment in the aftermath of World War I and built it into a national policy, especially after he came to power in 1933. The Nazis moved the Jewish people into confined ghettos, seized their property, and finally moved them into concentration camps such as Dachau. The initial Nazi plan was to move all nonessential Jewish people to Israel, but with the Allies controlling the Mediterranean Sea, the plan never materialized. Instead, young healthy Jewish men and women were used as slave labor. Most others, such as elderly Jews and children, were systematically killed.

What is shocking about the Holocaust is that all of the rest of the world made little attempt to save the Jewish people from being exterminated. The major Catholic and Protestant Church leaders across the world were silent as the Nazis began their killing. The United States even refused to allow a large passenger ship full of hundreds of Jewish refugees to enter the United States and turned it back to Germany. A few brave individuals from many nationalities—Germans, Danes, Dutch, and French—quietly hid Jewish children and friends from the Nazis. One of the few countries to openly accept Jewish refugees throughout the war was the Muslim country of Turkey (which had also accepted Jewish refugees fleeing the Christians in Spain in 1492). The state of Israel in 1947—after World War II—was set up as a reaction to the Nazi Holocaust so that the Jewish people could set up their own homeland.

- Quick Write: In a short paragraph, describe in your own words why other people all too often will not come to someone's assistance when he or she is in trouble.
- Bumper Sticker: Create a 1942 bumper sticker condemning the political and religious leaders of the world for not coming to the assistance of the Jewish people being exterminated by the Nazis.

- Free verse: In a free verse poem or a rap, criticize the world for not coming to the aid of the Jewish people during World War II.
- Time Traveler: In your class time machine, travel back to Istanbul, Turkey, in 1942 to interview Muhammad Mustafi (a student in costume). Muhammad is proud of the fact that despite the religious differences between Jewish people and Muslims, Muslim Turkey has openly accepted Jewish refugees from Christian Europe ever since the Middle Ages, including Nazi Germany during World War II.
- Action Research: As a class research project, ask grandparents and elderly neighbors what they remember about the Nazi Holocaust. Ask them also why church and political leaders did not come to the assistance of the Jewish people during the war.
- ADV Historical Research: Visit or write to a Holocaust Museum to find out what memories are being kept of the Nazi Holocaust and why it is important to keep such horrible memories.

7.8.2 Apartheid

In 1948, a pro-Nazi political party of Afrikaners (white Dutch-speaking farmers), the Nationalist Party, came to power in South Africa. Their stated goal was "white supremacy." Their plan of "apartheid" was to legally separate South Africa by ethnic groups to ensure "white supremacy." South Africa had 2.5 million people of European ancestry and over 11 million Africans in the country. Every African—of African ancestry—in the country had to carry an ethnic identity card, which treated them as foreigners in their own country, and made them legal for arrest at any time. It became illegal for people of European ancestry and African ancestry to marry each other. Children of European ancestry were allowed to go to school for free, while African children had to pay for their schooling. African children could only be schooled in their own language and not English. Any person who opposed the government was labeled a "communist."

One of the major people opposed to apartheid was Nelson Mandela (1918–), a South African lawyer and leader of the African National Congress (ANC). He was arrested and sent to prison in 1954 for organizing attacks against the Afrikaner-led South African government. By 1990, the pressure of world economic boycotts had turned against South Africa; President Frederik de Klerk (1936–) convinced his Nationalist Party to move toward the principle of majority rule by the

ANC. Nelson Mandela, after twenty-seven years, was released from prison. Apartheid was repealed and Nelson Mandela—a black African—was elected as the president of South Africa in 1994. His first words when elected were: "Never, never, and never again shall this beautiful land experience the oppression of one by another."

- Quick Write: In a short paragraph, describe how you would feel it you were put in jail for twenty-seven years because of the color of your skin. When you got out of jail, would you be angry or forgiving?
- Bumper Sticker: As a supporter of Nelson Mandela during the 1960s, create a bumper sticker calling for his release from prison.
- Personal Journal: As a black South African during the 1960s, describe what it feels like to have no political rights in your own country, to have to pay for school while white South African students do not, and not be allowed to work in a high-paying job.
- Brick Layer: (true story) According to South African apartheid rules, black South African bricklayers were allowed only to lay straight rows of bricks (for a minimum wage) and white South African bricklayers were allowed to lay only corner layers of bricks (for a much higher wage). With a student partner, create an imaginary conversation between a black South African bricklayer and a white South African bricklayer during the apartheid era and present it to your class when finished.
- Front Page: With a team of four student editors, create a front-page edition of the *Digital Times* focusing on apartheid in South Africa. Be sure to interview white Afrikaner and black African leaders (students in your class) about the nature of apartheid in South Africa and the unification of South Africa under Nelson Mandela.
- ADV Historical Research: Using your school library and the Internet, look for other examples of nation-states that discriminated against other ethnic groups and what eventually happened to these nation-states.

7.9.0   EXPLORATION AND DISCOVERY

7.9.1   The Quantum Universe

Sir Isaac Newton is wrong. The universe is *not* a mechanical model of fixed forces operating in a machine. The discovery that Newton's model was wrong was one of the major discoveries of the twentieth century. Just before the turn of the century, in 1897, Sir Joseph Thomas discovered the first atomic particle—the electron—and thereby created a new branch of physics: atomic physics. He proved that the world was made of atoms and that atoms had even smaller entities. In 1900, the German Max Planck discovered Newton's mistake. Planck found that atoms are not fixed, but are rather constantly changing by both absorbing and emitting radiant energy. Planck, in one discovery, destroyed Newton's fixed machine model of the universe.

In 1905, a brilliant twenty-six-year-old German by the name of Albert Einstein wrote three articles in which he first described the new quantum universe. Second, he verified Planck's theory by describing how light was emitted by quantum bursts (and not in a constant flow as described by Newton). Third, he showed that space and time are not absolute, but are forever changing (the theory of relativity). The only constant, said Einstein, was the speed of light. An object approaching the speed of light shortens in length, increases in mass, and slows in time. At the speed of light, everything has zero length, infinite mass, and time would cease to exist. In place of Newton's machine model of the universe was a relative quantum model of a universe in constant change (Gribbin 1984).

- Quick Write: In a short paragraph, describe a wave as it hits the beach or how a cloud changes as it moves across the sky. Now describe a crane lifting a piece of steel and placing it on a new bridge. What is the difference between your two descriptions? Which is a better description of our world? When finished, share your thoughts with the class.
- T Chart: On a T chart, compare Einstein's and Newton's views of the world.
- Poster Power: In a poster, compare Planck's and Einstein's quantum universe with Newton's mechanical universe from 300 years earlier.
- Bumper Sticker: Create a bumper sticker for space promoting Einstein's view of the universe.
- What If?: What if Einstein and Newton happened to meet in your classroom? What would they say to each other? What questions would you ask them? Dress two students as Sir Isaac (Newton) and Albert (Einstein) and have them be the two famous scientists meeting with your class. Every student in the class should also prepare at least one question to ask these famous scientists.
- ADV Historical Comparison: Using your library and the Internet, compare the discoveries of Planck and Einstein during the twentieth

century to the discoveries of Copernicus and Galileo 500 years earlier. How are their discoveries similar and different from each other? When finished, report your findings to the class.

- ADV The Futurist: Imagine a quantum human world in which people interacted peacefully with each other and continually played, worked, and changed without fighting. How would such a world be different from that of today? Interview three other classmates to see what they would think of such a quantum world of the future, and report your findings to the class.

7.9.2   Marconi: The First Radio Transmission (1901)

Lord Kelvin, perhaps the major scientist in the world in 1900, stated: "Radio has no future." Scientists knew that they could transmit sound by electricity by the late nineteenth century—but they could only do it for several yards. It took a sharp young Italian by the name of Guglielmo Marconi to discover how radio waves work. He did it in a grand way on December 12, 1901, at twelve noon. John Fleming sat in Cornwall, England, with an electric transmitter and tapped out the letter "s" (.) in Morse code. In St. Johns, Newfoundland, Marconi sat with a receiver almost 1,800 miles away. Almost instantly Marconi heard "." on his receiver. Marconi and Fleming had just made one of the major discoveries of the twentieth century—radio waves can be transmitted a very long way. Marconi's discovery was very simple—a grounded electrical antenna. With such grounded antenna attached to both the transmitter and receiver, radio sounds could be sent through the air. The larger the antenna, the longer the radio waves are and the longer they can be sent. In Newfoundland, Marconi attached his antenna to a kite flying several hundred feet in the air to receive the signal from Fleming in England. Thankfully, Lord Kelvin was wrong and Marconi was right (*Our Times* CD-ROM).

- Quick Write: Think of the last time you heard someone say: "It can never be done!" In a short paragraph, describe something you know has happened in your lifetime that people said could never happen. When finished, share your experience with the class.
- Poster Power: Create a poster celebrating Marconi's great achievement in 1901.
- Quick Skit: With a team of four student actors, create a short skit that illustrates the importance of Marconi's discovery.

- What if?: What if Marconi never discovered the grounded antenna? Make a list of your favorite songs and personalities you hear on the radio. When finished, describe in a letter to a friend what it would be like living without a radio.
- Time Traveler: Using your famous time machine, have Marconi (a student in costume) come and visit your classroom. Every student should prepare a question ahead of time to ask the discoverer of long distance radio waves.
- ADV Historical Comparison: Compare Marconi's discovery with other great discoveries in history. When finished, report your findings to your class.

7.9.3   DNA (1953)

James Watson was a sharp young American microbiologist (Ph.D. at age twenty-two). Francis Crick was a slightly older British biophysicist. Together, in 1953 they figured out how DNA worked. Since 1869, it had been known that deoxyribonucleic acid (DNA) was crucial to understanding how living cells duplicated themselves and passed along common genetic traits such as eye color, ear shape, and even transmit inherited genetic diseases. Watson and Crick made a great team. They were new to the study of DNA and they were not afraid of new ideas. They were not afraid to make mistakes. They were also willing to fully share ideas with each other, argue with each other, and criticize each other. The problem of DNA was a difficult one and they could not come up with the answer. Suddenly, while on a short vacation, Watson had a flash of brilliance. DNA had the same hourglass shape as the females he was watching on the beach. Quickly, Watson and Crick realized that DNA was composed of a double spiraling helix of two long strands of chromosomes. Each chromosome on the DNA double helix was responsible for a single genetic trait. When the DNA split, it became the basis of a new double helix. Now it was clear why a human being's cells are constantly dividing and replacing themselves and yet the person still looks the same and retains the same memories. The DNA discovery of Watson and Crick led to the replication of DNA in the test tube in 1967, the creation of artificial genes in 1976, and the cloning of a sheep in 1997. Biogeneticists working with the DNA molecule to replace disease-causing genes, improve physical performance, and maybe even clone human beings will be major issues and events throughout the twenty-first century. It was the discovery of Watson and Crick in 1953 that began these discoveries (*Our Times* CD-ROM).

- Quick Write: In a short paragraph, describe what you think it takes to come up with a great discovery that will change the world. When finished, share your ideas with the class.
- Poster Power #1: On a large poster, make a list of the things that Watson and Crick did together that made their team successful in discovering the structure of the DNA molecule.
- Poster Power #2: Using a science book or an encyclopedia, create an illustration of the structure of the DNA molecule discovered by Watson and Crick. Be sure to label critical elements of the molecule and share your work with the class.
- Quick Skit: With a partner, create a quick skit that illustrates the discovery of the structure of the DNA molecule by Watson and Crick.
- The Futurist: Each student should talk to parents, neighbors, and friends to make a list of genetic discoveries they would like to see in the future based on Watson and Crick's discovery.
- ADV Historical Analysis: Look back into history to identify how many possible things could have been changed if the discovery of the structure of the DNA molecule had happened much earlier. Be sure to share your observations with the class.

7.10.0 INVENTION AND REVOLUTION

The inventions and subsequent revolutions created during the twentieth century were numerous. Below are nine major inventions of the twentieth century. The class may be divided into teams, with each team charged with developing a full presentation on one particular invention and its implications for humans. Before their presentation, each team should use the library and the Internet to find out more about their invention.

Each team presentation should consist of the following items:

- Quick Write: Before each presentation, the team should have the members of the class each write a short paragraph describing what they know about the invention.
- Bumper Sticker: The invention team should have one or more members create a bumper sticker for the classroom wall celebrating the birth of this invention.

- Poster Power: The invention team should put together a poster that illustrates the importance of the invention to life during the twentieth century.
- Quick Skit: The invention team should create and present a short skit demonstrating the invention and what people first thought about it.
- The Futurist: The invention team should lead a class discussion on what is likely going to happen to the invention during the twenty-first century.

7.10.1   The Movies (1900)

Short, funny little movies on black-and-white film were being produced in the late nineteenth century nickelodeons. The first movie, however, to tell a real story was *Cinderella*—produced in 1900 by the Frenchman George Melies. Many film historians consider *The Great Train Robbery* (1903) to be the first real movie because of its length and because it was edited with numerous different camera shots and scenes. Whatever film was the first, by the first three years of the new century, movies were the new rage across the world and especially the United States.

7.10.2   The Airplane (1903)

Two bicycle builders from Ohio by the names of Orville and Wilber Wright traveled each year to Kitty Hawk, North Carolina, to test their new glider and motorized glider designs. In the strong steady wind of Kitty Hawk on December 17, 1903, the Wright brothers flew their flimsy motorized glider made of wood struts, wire, and cotton cloth for an amazing fifty-nine seconds in the air at fifteen feet above the ground before it crash-landed. They had just invented the first successful motorized airplane. The newspapers of the day, however, barely covered the event—but airplanes were now a reality.

7.10.3   The Automobile (1903)

A Detroit automaker by the name of Ransom P. Olds shattered automobile records by producing 3,000 "Oldsmobiles" in 1903. In the same year, a thin farmer's son from Michigan by the name of Henry Ford started his own automobile factory. Suddenly, automobiles were the rage. Horse owners hated them. They were noisy, dangerous, and dirty—but, boy, were they fun! In 1907, Ford created the Model T and made it into the major car in the world.

7.10.4 The Rocket (1926)

Some unknown scientist in China about 1000 C.E. invented the first gunpowder rocket; Rodger Bacon was working with such rockets two hundred years later. The first modern, liquid-fueled rocket for high-altitude flights, however, was invented by Robert Goddard, an American, in 1926. Most people in the United States ignored his work. Werner von Braun, however, the head of Germany's rocket program, was an avid reader of Goddard's work and incorporated it into the infamous Nazi rockets that were launched against England during World War II. Von Braun later became the head of the rocket program of the United States.

7.10.5   The Computer (1930)

In 1886, Herman Hollerith wished to speed up his tabulation of United States census data and created a method of punching holes into cards that could then be scanned by an electronic machine. It became the world's first computer. The first powerful, mechanical, analog computer, however, was constructed by Vannevar Bush at the Massachusetts Institute of Technology (MIT) in 1930. It took up over 200 square feet of floor space in a vacant room at MIT and every calculation had to be preset by turning hundreds of screws and hammering different levers. It was a far cry from the modern laptop computer, but it was a large first step.

7.10.6   TV (1941)

Modern commercial television was born on July 1, 1941, when David Sarnoff's National Broadcasting Corporation (NBC) and William Paley's Columbia Broadcasting System (CBS) began broadcasting fifteen hours per week of cartoons, news, and sports from New York City. The first regularly scheduled television, however, was broadcast from Nazi Germany in 1935, followed by the British Broadcasting Corporation in 1936. The United States was not too far behind; by 1939, twenty private television stations broadcast regularly in different cities. In the same year of 1939, NBC hired its first sports broadcaster—Red Barber—who pushed Procter and Gamble soap and Wheaties cereal between innings of national baseball games.

7.10.7   The Transistor (1947)

William Shockley created an electronic revolution in his Bell lab when he invented the transistor in 1947. Before his invention, electronic on and off switches could only be done by large, very hot vacuum tubes that often overheated and attracted lots of flying insects, which shorted out early computers (hence the origin of the term "computer bugs"). Shockley's small transistor switches were cool, efficient, and rarely broke down. They were a blessing to the computer industry—large computers that once filled whole rooms could now be shrunk to very small sizes. The popular press of the day, such as the *New York Times,* gave little notice to this major invention.

7.10.8   Space Travel: Sputnik (1957)

On October 4, 1957, the Soviet Union (Russia) launched a small, artificial satellite into orbit around the planet Earth. The name of the Russian satellite was called Sputnik. The United States at the time had a small rocket program with no interest in expanding it. Suddenly, however, their cold-war rival Russia had a satellite in space. Suddenly, there was a race for space between the United States and the USSR. In 1961, Russia launched its first astronaut into orbit. Space became a national obsession with both countries.

7.10.9   Microprocessors (1971)

The invention of the transistor in 1947 paved the way for the modern computer, but it was greatly helped along the way by the invention of the integrated circuit during the 1960s. In such integrated circuits, very small transistors, diodes, and resistors could be stamped into nonconducting silicon boards and connected with thin strips of silver. Such integrated circuits were stable, cool, and very powerful. By 1971, integrated circuits could be combined so efficiently that the whole computer could be placed on a fingernail. These new fingernail-sized computers were called microprocessors, and they paved the way for computer applications to be added to automobiles, telephones, airplanes, and virtually any conceivable electronic application.

7.11.0   ART AND CREATIVE THOUGHT

7.11.1   Cubism—Invented or Stolen?

Pablo Picasso (1881–1973) is credited with "inventing" cubism and twentieth-century abstract art in 1907 with his painting *Les Demoiselles d'Avignon (The Ladies of Avignon Street in Barcelona)*, now at the Museum of Modern Art in New York City. The Renaissance of the fifteenth century was famous for its realistic paintings by da Vinci and others who textured the colors of their painting and used shadows to make their work realistic. The impressionists of the nineteenth century, such as Claude Monet, used flat, bright colors to give an "impression" of a bridge or the ocean at dusk. The cubists, such as Picasso, forgot

Illustration 7.11.1   *Maconde Cubism from Tanzania, Africa*

about realism completely and how beautiful something looked to the eye. Instead, the cubists sought to paint images for the mind—not the eye. Cubist art divided up a subject into different fragmented and overlapping geometric plains, as if painting a person from different angles all at the same time.

Cubists such as Picasso revolutionized art in the twentieth century and made it abstract. In turn, the cubist movement also influenced sculpture, architecture, literature, and music throughout the twentieth century. Did Picasso really invent "cubism?" Picasso, himself, admits that he got the idea for cubism from African art. The African art he was referring to was the traditional abstract sculpture of the Makonde people of northeastern Tanzania. The Makonde for hundreds of years have carved their traditional sculptures of intertwined faces and bodies in different geometric shapes and from different angles. What do you think? Should Picasso really be given credit for creating cubism or should the Makonde people of Africa share in the credit (Boorstin 1992, 727–738)?

- Quick Write: If you were going to make a painting of the three most important times in your life, what would these three times be? Write a short paragraph, describing what these three times would look like in your painting.
- Map Attack: On a blank map of the world, indicate where Picasso made his first cubist painting in Barcelona, Spain, and where the Makonde made their traditional cubist statues in Tanzania, Africa. How far apart are these two centers of art?
- Venn Diagram: Compare one of Picasso's cubist paintings with a piece of Makonde art from Tanzania. Using a Venn diagram, indicate the unique features of each as well as the similar characteristics of both forms of art.
- Quick Skit: Imagine what would happen if Pablo Picasso met a traditional Makonde woodcarver named Neyerre. What would they say to each other? How would they act with each other? With a partner, create a short skit that illustrates what might have happened if the two really met. When ready, share your skit with the class.
- Western Art Mart: Create a drawing in the cubist style of Picasso and share it with your class.
- African Art Mart: Create a drawing in the traditional abstract style of Makonde people of Tanzania and share it with your class.
- ADV Historical Comparison: Cubist "art" by Picasso today is worth millions of dollars while an African Makonde piece of "cubist"

sculpture (from where Picasso got his ideas) is often labeled as "craft" (not "art") and sold for only a few dollars in local African shops. Explore the difference between European "art" and African "crafts." Why does European "art" cost so much money and why are African "crafts" so cheap?

7.11.2   That's Jazz!

When asked to define jazz, Louis Armstrong (one of the founders of jazz) answered: "Man, if you gotta ask, you'll never know." Jazz—as a musical form—emerged during the twentieth century in New Orleans, Louisiana, from its African American roots in nineteenth-century work songs and spirituals. Slowly, it moved up the Mississippi River to Memphis, Kansas City, and Chicago, and then spread across the United States. Although many of its roots were in Africa and its instruments were European, jazz was a purely twentieth-century American creation that spread rapidly around the world. Because of its African American origins, jazz did not immediately catch on with most European Americans. Europeans, for the first half of the twentieth century, were more enthusiastic about jazz than European Americans, and as a result, many African American jazz musicians lived in Europe.

Blues was the heart of jazz with "blue" flattened third and seventh notes to distinguish its sound. It was the sound of poor and hard-working African Americans trying to do the best they could. The words of jazz dealt with love, poverty, and death and were earthy and direct. Jelly Roll Morton (1885–1941) was one of the first jazz musicians, as was Louis Armstrong (1900–1971). Several people and institutions slowly introduced jazz to the white American public. The first was the famous Cotton Club in Harlem, New York, where famous black bands such as Duke Ellington and Count Basie played to packed "white only" audiences during the 1920s. Second was George Gershwin, a Jewish boy who lived in black-dominated Harlem, who wrote such masterpieces as *Rhapsody in Blue* and popularized jazz across much of white America. Third were Benny Goodman, whose swing band of the late 1930s began to use black performers, Lionel Hampton, and Billie Holiday, who spread the hot sound of jazz to all Americans and everyone around the world. The twentieth century was dominated by the United States, and the musical idiom of jazz certainly contributed culturally to this dominance (Schiller 1968).

- Quick Write: Close your eyes for a minute. When you hear the word "jazz," what do you see? In a short paragraph, describe what you see with the word "jazz" and then share your impressions with the class.
- Bumper Sticker: Create a bumper sticker from the early twentieth century celebrating the birth of jazz.
- Poster Power: Create a poster advertising the famous jazz hot spot—the Cotton Club—in African American–dominated Harlem in 1929 when Duke Ellington and his orchestra were playing to packed "whites only" audiences.
- Demo: Invite a local musician to your class to have him or her demonstrate how and why jazz is different from classical European music.
- Jazz Day: Pick a day to become "Jazz Day" at your school. Students should wear 1930s clothes. History classes will be devoted to listening to and comparing the jazz sounds of Louis Armstrong, Duke Ellington, Benny Goodman, and Miles Davis. English classes will focus on the writings of Harlem Renaissance writers such as Langston Hughes. Student and faculty musicians at school can demonstrate some early twentieth-century jazz music. A 1930s swing jazz dance could be held after school.
- ADV Historical Analysis: Research your library and the Internet to determine why jazz—an American creation—was popular in Europe before it was in the United States. When finished, share your findings with the class.

7.11.3   Marxist Anarchy: *Duck Soup* (1933)

The Marx Brothers had absolutely nothing to do with Karl Marx! In fact, they were almost the exact opposite of the deadly serious politics and economics of Karl—they were never serious, and always made fun of anybody who was serious. In Paramount Pictures' 1933 film *Duck Soup,* Rufus T. Firefly (Groucho Marx) was the president of Freedonia and was having problems with his minister of war (Anobile 1971, 162–162):

> **Minister of War:** Gentlemen, Gentlemen! Enough of this. How about taking up the tax?
> **Firefly:** How about taking up the carpet?
> **Minister of War:** I still insist we must take up the tax!
> **Firefly:** He's right. You've got to take up the tacks before you take up the carpet.
> **Minister of War:** I give all my time and energy to my duties and what do I get?

Firefly: You get awfully tiresome after a while.

Minister of War: Sir! You try my patience!

Firefly: I do not mind if I do! You must come over and try some of mine sometime.

Minister of War: That's the last straw! I resign. I wash my hands of the whole business.

Firefly: A good idea. You can wash your neck, too!

Everybody in the world laughed at the wacko comedy of movies of the Marx Brothers during the 1930s. Well, almost everybody except for the fascists in Italy under Mussolini and the Nazis in Germany under Adolf Hitler. The fascists and the Nazis banned the Marx Brothers' films in Italy and Germany because they did not like being laughed at and also because the Marx Brothers were Jewish. The Marx Brothers responded with their own unwritten rule: "Never trust a politician who cannot laugh at himself!"

- Quick Write: In a short paragraph, tell the funniest story you know.
- Readers' Theater: Divide the class into pairs of students and have each pair read the above script out loud to each other, as fast as they can without making a mistake. The Marx Brothers never recited their lines slowly. Have a competition between the pairs of students as to the best and funniest pair of readers.
- Poster Power: Using the above script from *Duck Soup*, create a poster advertising this riotous Marx Brothers' film.
- Quick Skit: Using the *Duck Soup* script (above) as a model in the style of the Marx Brothers, have pairs of students create short skits that make fun of serious politicians, teachers, or school administrators and present them to the class.
- Front Page: In a team of four student editors, create a front-page edition of the *Digital Times* focusing on the fascist and Nazi opposition to the Marx Brothers' films. Be sure to include interviews with Mussolini, Hitler, and the Marx Brothers themselves concerning the banned films.
- Action Research: Have students in the class interview parents, grandparents, and relatives about their joyful memories of the Marx Brothers' films.
- Check It Out: The next time you are at a video store, rent one of the Marx Brothers' films, view it at home with your family, and then give an oral report to your class on the film.

- ADV Research Project: Use your library and the Internet to research the importance of comedy in dealing with serious political problems and report your findings to the class.

7.12.0 SUCCESSES AND FAILURES OF THE TWENTIETH CENTURY

7.12.1 Women's Suffrage (1903)

When will women receive the full political rights of men? Emmeline Pankhurst (1858–1928) asked this question in 1903 when she founded the Woman's Social and Political Union in England. Emmeline, her husband Richard, and her daughters Christabel and Sylvia believed in forcing the men of England to let women vote—they clipped telegraph wires, burned down old deserted buildings, and generally heckled any politician who did not believe in women's rights. The police often arrested her, but when they did, she refused to eat in jail, or pay any fine, and so they released her. Pankhurst, in reality, was the follower of the leader of the suffrage movement in the United States, Susan B. Anthony (1820–1906). In 1872, Anthony led a group of women to attempt to vote in the election of that year. She was arrested but refused to cooperate with her jailers, and refused to pay any fine for her actions. New Zealand, Finland, and Norway gave women the right to vote before World War I. Russia (the new Soviet Union under Lenin) granted women the right to vote in 1917, followed by England and Canada and most of Europe shortly afterward. Slowly and reluctantly, the United States followed the example of Europe and gave women the right to vote with the passage of the Nineteenth Amendment in 1920 (Harper 1969).

- Quick Write: In a short paragraph, give your opinion as to whether or not you think that females should have the same rights as males.
- Bumper Sticker: Create a bumper sticker for an early automobile that supports women's equal rights to those of men.
- Counter Bumper Sticker: Create a bumper sticker for an early Model T Ford that opposes equal rights for men and women.
- Poster Power: Create a large poster for your classroom wall that depicts the early struggle for women's rights.
- T Chart: Create a T chart that compares the rights of men and the rights of women.

- Quick Skit: With a team of four student actors from class, create a short skit that depicts the early women's rights movements and the opposition of many men to giving women the same rights they enjoyed.
- ADV The Futurist: Conduct a poll of your classmates, teachers, and parents to see when they believe the United States will elect a female to be president of the United States.

7.12.2 Versailles (1919)

World War I was over (1919). The Allies—England, France, and the United States—had won; Germany and its allies were the losers. They all met at the French Palace of Versailles to sign a peace treaty. The Peace Treaty of Versailles ended World War I, but it did not turn out to be a treaty of peace; instead, it resulted in a treaty that became one of the major causes of World War II twenty years later. Woodrow Wilson, the idealistic president of the United States, came to Versailles with a plan to make peace between the major powers of Europe for all time with the creation of a League of Nations. Very quickly, however, it became evident that this was not going to be a peace for all time. Lloyd George, the British prime minister, and Clemenceau, the French premiere, had other plans. Both the English and the French refused to let the Germans be at the peace conference. It soon became clear that France's major goal at the conference was to get revenge against Germany and England's major goal was to strengthen its colonial empire. Wilson left Versailles a defeated man; he got a very weak League of Nations, but little else. England and France, on the other hand, were given control of the major former German colonies as League of Nations mandates. England and France were also winners in that they got a provision in the treaty that forced Germany to pay reparations for their costs of the war. Germany was forced to sign the treaty without any negotiation. France and England left Versailles happy. Germany, on the other hand, was quite angry. Many English and French colonies were also angry; they had fought hard for the colonial government during the war and expected freedom when it was finished. They did not get it. The German anger at how they were treated at Versailles contributed to World War II twenty years later.

- Quick Write: In a short paragraph, describe a time in your life when you felt you were cheated. What happened as a result of this incident?

- Poster Power: Have four people in your class each create a poster that illustrates the viewpoint of Germany, the United States, England, or France at the conclusion of the Treaty of Versailles.
- Map Attack: On a blank map of the world, illustrate the major countries that were at Versailles and what they gained or lost at Versailles.
- Quick Skit: In a team of four students, create a short skit that illustrates a discussion between a German, an American, a French person, and an English person about the meaning of Versailles.
- Poet's Corner: Create an epic free verse poem about the problems encountered at Versailles and what they meant to the world.
- ADV Historical Research: Compare the peace conference at Versailles with other major peace conferences, such as the Conference of Vienna that ended the Napoleonic War in 1814. What similarities and differences existed between these treaties? When completed, share your findings with the class.
- ADV What If?: What if you were at Versailles? What changes would you make to ensure the peace of Europe and the World for a long time? In a team of four, develop your own plans for a treaty to end World War I and then present your conclusions to the class when finished.

7.12.3   The United Nations (1944)

Does the world need an international organization to keep the peace? This was the major question that President Wilson from the United States brought to the Versailles Peace Conference at the end of World War I. Although Wilson obtained very little of what he wanted from the conference, he did obtain a "League of Nations" that could work toward maintaining peace in the world. The United States Senate, however, refused to ratify the Treaty of Versailles that created the League of Nations. Many senators, led by Henry Cabot Lodge, were isolationists who did not want the United States to be involved any more in European politics and warfare. Wilson died trying to get United States' support for his League of Nations. The United States' refusal to join the League also doomed it to failure at stopping any world conflict, such as World War II twenty years later.

The United Nations was created in 1944, during World War II, with the same hope of maintaining world peace. Since World War II, the United Nations has intervened in literally hundreds of international disputes and provided a neutral force to stop the fighting. It has provided assistance to millions of refugees fleeing wars around the world, and it has provided a forum for the many nations of the world to resolve their differences. Many times during the late twentieth century, the United Nations has been unable to act because its major members—the United States and the Soviet Union—disagreed about what to do. With the growing power of the United States across the world, many in the United States oppose the United Nations because they think it interferes with what the United States wants. The question for the twenty-first century is whether or not the United Nations should be given more power over individual countries—such as the United States—to prevent future international conflicts from occurring (Waters 1967).

- Quick Write: In a short paragraph, state your opinion whether or not you think the planet Earth should be ruled by a "united federation of states" designed to keep world peace, or whether individual nations should be allowed to fight wars with each other.
- T Chart: Using a T chart, compare the world united under one peaceful government with another world in which individual governments are allowed to fight wars with each other.
- Pair Share: With a partner, have each speak one minute on their opinion concerning the need, or lack of it, for an international organization such as the United Nations.
- Front Page: With a team of four student editors, create a front-page edition of the *Digital Times*—the leading cyber newspaper of the twentieth century—reviewing the accomplishments and failures of the United Nations since its founding in 1944. You can use your library and the Internet as sources of information on the topic.
- Quick Skit: With four student actors from your class, create and present to your class a short skit illustrating the debate whether the United Nations should be made into a world government or whether individual countries, such as the United States, should continue to make their own decisions regarding war and peace in the world.
- The Futurist: Imagine what it would be like to live under a world government in the future. Write a short paragraph about what you would like and dislike about this type of government.
- ADV Historical Comparison: Using your school library and the Internet as resources, compare the successes and failures of the League of Nations and the United Nations during the twentieth century. What conclusions can you draw from the comparisons between these two organizations?

7.12.4 The Atomic Bomb (1945)

Should the United States have dropped the atomic bombs on Hiroshima and Nagasaki in Japan at the end of World War II?

Time stopped for a moment in Hiroshima, Japan, at 8:15 A.M. on August 6, 1945. An atomic blast froze all clocks in Hiroshima to that specific time. The same blast instantly vaporized 80,000 people and later killed another 140,000 people through radiation poisoning and birth defects. Four days later, a second atomic blast occurred in Nagasaki, Japan, instantly killing another 40,000 people. The United States of America had just dropped two new horrible inventions of war—atomic bombs—on Japan. On August 14th, four days later, Japan surrendered, ending World War II.

A raging debate in history has been whether or not the United States needed to drop the atomic bombs on Japan to end World War II. Almost every history textbook says that Japan surrendered because it feared that the United States was going to drop more atomic bombs. President Harry Truman's speech on August 7th seems to support this view: "Sixteen hours ago, an American airplane dropped one bomb on Hiroshima. If they do not now accept our terms, they may expect a rain of ruin from the sky the likes of which has never been seen on this earth" (*Our Times* CD-ROM 1995).

The simple chronology of events before the surrender also seems to support this, but many other pieces of historical information do not fit this interpretation. Unofficial discussions about surrender were taking place between the United States and Japan before the dropping of the atomic bombs. The United States insisted on unconditional surrender while Japan insisted on retaining the emperor if it surrendered. Japan surrendered on August 14th only after the United States agreed that Japan could keep its emperor. A second important fact is that the Soviet Union declared war on Japan on August 8th—as agreed to earlier with the United States and two days after the atomic bomb was dropped on Hiroshima. Was the United States using the atomic bomb to intimidate the Russians in a first act of the Cold War? Or did the United States just want to test its powerful new weapon in wartime, before the end of the war in a few days? The historical debate on this topic continues.

- Quick Write: In a short paragraph, describe whether you—as the president of the United States—would try to end a war peacefully or would you end it with a show of force?

- Bumper Sticker: Create a bumper sticker for 1945 either supporting or opposing the use of the atomic bomb against the Japanese in World War II.
- Pair Share: With a partner in class, each talk for one minute expressing your views on whether or not the United States should have dropped its two atomic bombs on Hiroshima.
- Poet's Corner: Create a poem or a rap focusing on the horror of the dropping of the atomic bomb on Hiroshima.
- You Were There: As host to this popular quiz show during the twentieth century, you use your time machine to transport your class to 1945 to interview four important guests concerning their views on the dropping of the atomic bomb on Hiroshima and Nagasaki. Be sure to have the students in your class ready with a minimum of two questions each to ask your important guests:
    1. Hirohito, emperor of Japan—the emperor is pleased that the United States finally agreed to let him continue in power after World War II and disagrees that the dropping of the atomic bombs had anything to do with the ending of the war.
    2. General Leslie Groves, in charge of building the atomic bomb— General Groves believes that the Japanese deserve every bomb the United States can throw at them, including the atomic bomb. He also really wants to see the bomb tested to see if it works in wartime.
    3. Lieutenant James Armstrong—Lieutenant Armstrong was to be one of the first soldiers leading the landing of U.S. troops on Japan. He believes firmly that the atomic bomb ended the war and saved the lives of millions of his men who would have had to fight the Japanese on their own island.
    4. Joseph Stalin, premiere of the Soviet Union—Stalin definitely thinks that the Japanese were ready to surrender before the dropping of the atomic bomb on Hiroshima. He also strongly believes that Truman deliberately dropped the bomb to intimidate Russia (the Soviet Union) in the first step of the Cold War between the United States and Russia.
- ADV Ethnic Controversy: A very sensitive issue of racism also plays into the question of the dropping of the bomb on Hiroshima. Would the United States have used the atomic bomb against Germany during World War II, if Germany had not surrendered before the atomic bomb was built? Was the United States willing to drop the atomic bomb on Japan because they were "Asian," but would not have dropped the

atomic bomb on Germany, because they were "European," just like most Americans? Research this volatile issue in your school library and on the Internet, and then report your findings to the class.

7.12.5   Silkworm: China's Rocket Program (1955)

During the 1950s, the United States underwent a period of national paranoia—called *the McCarthy era*—in which the great fear existed that communists were taking over the country. The extremes paranoia that gripped the nation is best illustrated by the story of Tsien Hsue-shen. Tsien Hsue-shen was born in China in 1911, but came to the United States to study physics at Cal Tech in Pasadena, California. He and four other Cal Tech students founded JPL (Jet Propulsion Laboratory), which became one of the first major centers for the study of missiles and rockets in the United States. He was soon recognized as one of the most important rocket scientists in the United States and the world during World War II. At the end of World War II, Tsien Hsue-shen was the major scientist who assisted the United States military in bringing the major men and materials of defeated Germany's rocket program to the United States. The FBI and other McCarthy followers suddenly realized that someone deep in the military missile program of the United States was Chinese and therefore might be "a communist." Hysterical paranoia of the era bypassed any reason. Tsien Hsue-shen was banned from working on any rocket programs for the United States military. In 1955, the United States government—locked into the McCarthy hysteria of the era—expelled Tsien Hsue-shen and his family (born in the United States) to the People's Republic of China. China, under the communist rule of Mao Ze-dong, had no rocket program in 1955. The United States had given Mao Ze-dong and Communist China one of the world's top rocket scientists. By the end of the twentieth century, the People's Republic of China under the leadership of Tsien Hsue-shen had created one of the major military missile and rocket programs in the world and a direct threat to the United States and the rest of Asia. Without the gift of Tsien Hsue-shen from the United States to China in 1955, China likely would not have been able to develop a large missile and rocket program during the twentieth century (Chang 1995).

- Quick Write: Think for a moment and then write a paragraph about the biggest mistake you ever made. What happened as a result of this mistake?

- Poster Power: With a partner, create a poster for your classroom wall that illustrates the extreme paranoia of the McCarthy "anticommunist" era.
- Share Pair: With a partner, each talk for one minute about the story of Tsien Hsue-shen and the "anticommunist" McCarthy era of the 1950s. What is the major lesson that we should learn from this incident? When finished, each team can share their ideas with the class.
- Quick Skit: In a team of four, create a short skit that illustrates the major blunders a country like the United States can make when it is driven by extreme paranoia, such as the McCarthy anticommunist hysteria of the 1950s.
- Action Research #1: Have students in the class interview older neighbors and relatives about the paranoid anticommunist hysteria of the McCarthy era. When finished, they can report to the class on their findings.
- Action Research #2: In the library and in video stores, find and report on old 1950s magazines, newspapers, and movies that illustrated the anticommunist paranoia of the 1950s in the United States.
- What If?: With a partner, recreate a scenario in which Tsien Hsue-shen is never expelled from the United States and sent to China. How would history have been changed?
- ADV Research Project: Using your library and the Internet, go back in history to find previous instances in history when extreme paranoia and racism have produced major blunders and tragedies in history (for example: the Nazi Holocaust of World War II).

7.13.0   MAJOR WORLD PROBLEMS FOR THE TWENTY-FIRST CENTURY

7.13.1   The Population Trap

Will the planet Earth have a human overpopulation problem during the twenty-first century? Table 7.13.1 shows the data needed to analyze and make some critical decisions concerning this potential major planetary problem. The data in table 7.13.1 lists the Earth's total population in five-year increments and how much it increased yearly between 1950 and 1995.

- Quick Write: In a short paragraph, describe what you think might happen if the world has too many people. When finished, share your ideas with the class.

Table 7.13.1   Planet Earth's Population Growth by Year

Year	Total Population (billion)	Annual Growth (millions)
1985	4.855	81
1990	5.282	87
1960	3.039	42
1950	2.556	37
1975	4.087	74
1995	5.691	81
1955	2.780	51
1970	3.706	75
1965	3.345	69
1980	4.458	77

(Source: Brown 1997, 81)

- Time Corrector: Place the data in chronological order by five-year increments: 1950–1995.
- Graph Master #1: On a large piece of paper, create a graph for your classroom wall that plots the population change of planet Earth between 1950 and 1995. (Place the five-year increments between 1950 and 1995 across the bottom of the page and the population scale—between two and eight billion—along the left side of the paper. See the example in table 7.13.1a.)
- Graph Master #2: On a similar graph, plot the *amount of change* in population growth (in millions) for each five-year period. The bottom yearly scale for this graph can remain the same, but the vertical scale to the left of the graph should be drawn between fifty million people (bottom) and ninety million people (top).
- Graph Analyzer: Now look carefully at both of the graphs you have created. In a short paragraph, describe what is happening to the pop-

Table 7.13.1a   Example Population Growth Chart

	1950	1955	1960	1965	1970	1975	1980	1985	1990	1995
7 billion										
6 billion										
5 billion										
4 billion										
3 billion										
2 billion										

ulation of the planet Earth, and then share your findings with the class.

- The Futurist #1: Combining the directions of the graphs, make a prediction for the population of the world in 2010 and 2050 (assuming that the population of the world will grow at a rate of eighty million per year).
- The Futurist #2: Create another graph for your classroom wall illustrating the population growth between 2000 and 2050 of the five largest countries in the world, using the data in table 7.13.1b.
- ADV Futurist #3: Can India, China, and Pakistan (the fastest growing countries in the world) take care of all their people in the future—in 2010 and 2050? What will they have to do to support their growing populations?

Table 7.13.1b   Data for Population Growth Chart

	2000	2050	
India	976 mil	1,533 mil	(use a solid line)
China	1,255 mil	1,517 mil	(use dashes for a line)
Pakistan	148 mil	357 mil	(use dots for a line)
United States	274 mil	348 mil	(use "o"s for a line)
Nigeria	122 mil	339 mil	(use "*"s for a line)

(Source: Brown 1998b, 10)

7.13.2   The Food Trap

Will there be enough food to feed the growing population of the world? Use the data in table 7.13.2 to analyze the whole problem of growing food for the billions of people in the world (Brown 1998b, 13–15, 31–33).

- Quick Write: Close your eyes for a moment and imagine a sad time in the future when you will have no food to eat for the next three days. In a short paragraph, describe how you will feel, what you will do, and what plans you will make for the future to ensure that you will have enough food.
- Time Corrector: Reorder the data in table 7.13.2 to place it in correct chronological order.
- Graph Master #1: On a large piece of paper for the classroom wall, graph the total grain production of the world (using the data in table 7.13.2) between the years 1950 and 1995.

Table 7.13.2   World Food Production: Total Production vs. Per Capita Production (1950–1995)

Year	Total Grain Population (millions of tons)	Per Capita Grain Production (kilograms)
1975	1,237	303
1990	1,767	335
1960	824	271
1995	1,703	299
1985	1,469	339
1950	631	247
1980	1,429	321
1970	1,079	291
1955	759	273
1965	904	270

(Source: Brown 1997, 26–27. See also Brown 1998a, 79–95.)

- Graph Master #2: On a large piece of paper for the classroom wall, graph the total per capita (per person) grain production of the world between the years 1950 and 1995 (using the data from table 7.13.2).
- Graph Analyzer: Using the two graphs, analyze the trends in total and per capita grain production in the world. In a short paragraph, write your conclusions about what the graphs are saying. When finished, share your conclusions with the class.
- The Futurist #1: Project these graphs out to the years 2010 and 2050. From these projections, what will be happening to the grain production of the world?
- ADV The Futurist #2: From research in the school library and on the Internet, make some major decisions to present to your class to solve the major problem of size of the increasing population of the world outpacing the ability of humans to grow more grain.

7.13.3   The Water Trap

Will there be enough fresh water for the planet Earth during the twenty-first century? The major aquifers supplying drinking water to major areas of the world are being overutilized and are drying up. Fresh water is in critical shortage in China, India, the Middle East, North Africa, and the southwestern United States. Analyze the data in table 7.13.3 to understand the seriousness of this problem and then make some crucial decisions about how the planet needs to handle this issue.

Table 7.13.3   The Fresh Water Trap

Irrigated Hectares of Global Farmland Per Person (1950–1995)	
1965	0.043 hectares per person
1995	0.042 hectares per person
1975	0.045 hectares per person
1980	0.048 hectares per person
1950	0.038 hectares per person
1985	0.046 hectares per person
1960	0.045 hectares per person
1990	0.045 hectares per person
1955	0.041 hectares per person
1970	0.044 hectares per person

(Source: Brown 1998b, 16–18)

- Quick Write: Go back for a moment and think of when you were without water for most of a day. In a short paragraph, describe how it felt to be without water. Imagine living your whole life without as much water as you would like and need. When finished, present your impressions to the class.
- Time Corrector: Reorganize the data in table 7.13.3 by year, indicating how much land per person is being irrigated across the planet.
- Graph Master: Create a large graph of the irrigation data in table 7.13.3 for the planet Earth between the years 1950 and 1995. When finished, present it to the class and hang it up on the classroom wall.
- Graph Analyzer: Studying the above world irrigation graph, what is happening to the fresh water across the world?
- Futurist #1: From the above graph, project how much irrigated land will be available per person in 2010 and 2050. In a short paragraph, describe the major problem you see and present your thoughts on this issue to the class.
- ADV Futurist #2: The reduced amount of irrigated land in use across the world is due to a large number of factors: more urban use of fresh water, aquifers drying up, and overirrigation leaving large salt deposits on the formerly good farm land. Using your library and the Internet, explore the problem of limited fresh water available for the future and report your findings to the class.

7.13.4   The Climate Trap

Is global warming a falsehood or a reality? If it is a reality, can humans do anything to correct it? Using the data from table 7.13.4, transform it into a chronologically based graph to analyze it, and begin to under-

Table 7.13.4   The Climate Trap

Average Global Temperatures by Year (1950–1995)	
1965	14.88 Degrees Celsius
1995	15.40 Degrees Celsius
1975	14.92 Degrees Celsius
1980	15.18 Degrees Celsius
1950	14.86 Degrees Celsius
1985	15.09 Degrees Celsius
1960	14.98 Degrees Celsius
1990	15.39 Degrees Celsius
1955	14.92 Degrees Celsius
1970	15.02 Degrees Celsius

(Source: Brown 1997, 62–63)

stand how serious this problem is (Brown 1998b, 22–24; Flavin and Dunn 1998, 113–130; Gardner 1998, 96–112).

- Quick Write: In a short paragraph, describe what you think might happen if the Earth starts to heat up—especially the polar ice caps. If the ice caps melt, what do you think will happen to all the low-lying cities and states, such as New York City and Florida, which are not very high above sea level? When finished, share your thoughts with your class.
- Time Corrector: Reorganize the data in table 7.13.4 to chronologically illustrate the temperature trend of the planet Earth.
- Graph Master: Create a large graph of the temperature data for the planet Earth between the years 1950 and 1995. When finished, present it to the class and display it in the class.
- Graph Analyzer: Studying the temperature graph, what is happening to the temperature across the world?
- Futurist #1: From the graph, project how much the average temperature of the Earth will rise or fall in 2010 and 2050. In a short paragraph, describe the major problem you see from your analysis and present your thoughts on it to the class.
- ADV Futurist #2: The industrialized countries of the world are greatly increasing their burning of fossil fuels for ever more automobiles and factories. This process is sending even greater amounts of pollution and heat into the atmosphere. Is this process causing the temperature of the planet to increase, or is the increase of temperature due to natural causes? Can the humans on our planet afford to wait to see if the temperature increase is human made or natural? Using your school library and the Internet, research the issue of global warming and report back to the class on your findings of what can be done.

7.13.5   The Poverty Trap

Should the people on planet Earth be concerned about the widening gap between the rich and the poor in the world? The Greek philosopher Plato, in his *Republic*, believed that the ideal was to have the richest people in society earn five times more than the poor. In 1961, according to the United Nations Development Program (UNDP), the richest 20 percent earned thirty times more than the poorest 20 percent of humanity across the world. In 1991, according to the same source, the richest 20 percent earned 61 times more than the poorest 20 percent of humanity.

The industrialized world is also rapidly moving away from the non-industrialized world with the wealth of the planet. Over 80 percent of the Earth's population lives in the nonindustrialized world and yet, out of the $23 trillion dollars in gross world product (in 1993), $18 trillion dollars was produced in industrialized countries such as the United States and only $5 trillion in the nonindustrialized world. The gap is increasing. The growing gap in per capita income between the industrialized and nonindustrialized countries almost tripled between the years 1960 and 1993, from $5,700 to $15,400.

The mineral wealth of much of the world lies in the nonindustrialized world. It is sold cheaply to the industrialized world that, in turn, changes it into manufactured goods and sells these goods back to the nonindustrialized countries at high prices.

The greatest gaps between the richest and the poorest people, however, lie in the nonindustrialized countries where a few individuals have been able to amass a great deal of wealth at the expense of the poor around them. Compare the difference in wealth between the richest and the poorest in the ten countries in table 7.13.5.

Table 7.13.5   Income Ratios of the Richest 20 Percent and the Poorest 20 Percent per Country

Country	Income Ratio	Country Type
Japan	4.3	Industrialized
Germany	5.8	Industrialized
United States	8.9	Industrialized
Russia	11.4	Industrialized
Vietnam	5.6	Nonindustrialized
Nigeria	9.6	Nonindustrialized
Chile	18.3	Nonindustrialized
South Africa	19.1	Nonindustrialized
Panama	29.9	Nonindustrialized
Brazil	32.1	Nonindustrialized

What is the result of this increasing distance between the rich and the poor around the world? Studies by Harvard and Cambridge Universities (in 1995) found that countries with higher income inequalities also had higher percentages of civil unrest and lower investment because of the fear of civil unrest. These studies may be an indicator of a major problem of the twenty-first century in countries where the distance between the rich and the poor is increasing (Brown et al. 1997, 116–117; French 1998, 149–167).

- Quick Write: In a short paragraph, describe the major differences you see between people who are rich and people who are poor.
- Bumper Sticker #1: As a rich person, create a bumper sticker that describes your view of the world.
- Bumper Sticker #2: As a poor person, create a bumper sticker that describes your view of the world.
- Poster Power: Create a poster for your class wall that illustrates the increasing gap between the rich and the poor in the world.
- Quick Skit: With a team of four students, create a short dramatization that illustrates the major problem of the increasing gap between the rich and the poor in the world.
- Front Page: With a team of four student editors, create a front-page edition of the *Digital Times* on-line newspaper that focuses on the increasing gap between the rich and the poor in the world. Be sure to interview people from all points of view on the subject and include an illustration that demonstrates this major world problem.
- ADV The Futurist: Using sources in your school library and on the Internet, identify major problems in trying to solve the income inequity problem across the world and present your findings to the class.

7.13.6   The War Trap

The human costs of war during the twentieth century were staggering. Fifty-six million people died in World War II alone. We can only begin to imagine the emotional costs of such wars on the families involved in the fighting. And the fighting continues. The University of Sweden counted 101 military conflicts during the brief seven-year period of 1989–1996, and almost all of these were armed struggles within individual countries, such as Angola, Afghanistan, Indonesia,

Israel, Lebanon, and Rwanda. The financial drain of warfare on the economies of the world is also staggering. Between 1946 (the end of World War II) and 1996, individual governments across the planet spent an estimated $30–35 trillion on new military weapons. The financial costs of warfare, however, are far greater than just military hardware. A small war, such as the Persian Gulf conflict of 1990–1991 with the Iraqi invasion of Kuwait and the subsequent counterattack, cost approximately $676 billion dollars in direct military costs; the damage to buildings, homes, and roads; the medical costs of the injured; the lost income of those caught by the war; the international flow of refugees fleeing from the fighting; and the staggering costs of rebuilding after such a war. Kuwait is a rich country with the finances to quickly rebuild after such a devastating war. The financial ability to rebuild after a war, however, is not available to poor, third-world countries such as Angola (total cost: $30 billion), El Salvador (total cost: $1.1 billion), Mozambique (total cost: $15 billion), and Nicaragua (total cost: $2.5 billion). The immense cost of land mine removal alone is beyond the reach of these poor nations. Such poor nations could take decades to recover from such wars.

Can wars around the planet be stopped during the twenty-first century? Yes, they can. It is estimated that for every $250 the governments of the planet spend on their militaries, they would only have to spend $1 dollar for peacekeeping to keep most of the conflicts of the world from turning into open wars (Renner 1994, 9). Politicians in many countries, however, oppose spending money for international peacekeeping because their economies benefit greatly from international sales of weapons—especially to poor countries. Post–Cold-War fighting is also done, not with nuclear weapons, but with small weapons. Fifty million dollars may only buy one jet fighter plane for Russia or the United States; for a small nation or group of terrorists, however, it will buy 200,000 used assault rifles from the United States, Russia, South Africa, or Israel. The world is awash in such weapons: seventy million Russian AK-47s, ten million Israeli Uzis, eight million M-1s from the United States, and seven million German G-3s. They are easy to acquire and easy to transport, and they are deadly. Yes, wars can be stopped, but it will take a concerted effort on the part of the governments of the world to spend money on peacekeeping and destroy—not sell—used weapons of war (Boulding 1964, 75–103; Renner 1994; Renner 1998, 131–148).

- Quick Write: Close your eyes for a moment and imagine you are caught in a war and you have no idea who is fighting or why. In a short paragraph, quickly write down what comes to your mind as you think about this war. When finished, describe your impressions to the class.
- Pair Share: With a fellow student, discuss what would happen if 100 automatic assault weapons and ammunition from an unknown source suddenly appeared in your town. What would people do with these guns? How would it change your town? Imagine what this would be like in towns in many poor countries in the world. Share your thoughts with your whole class.
- Music Mart: With a fellow student, create a poem, a rap, or a song about your impressions of war and then share it with your class.
- Bumper Sticker: Create a bumper sticker to present to your class and then to the United Nations that illustrates your feelings about war.
- Poster Power: With a team of four students, create a poster that illustrates both the human and financial costs that modern warfare has had on the countries of the world.
- Pros and Cons: With a partner, create a short skit that illustrates both being in favor of a war and being opposed to a war.
- Front Page: With a team of four students, create a front-page edition of the *Digital Times* newspaper that looks at the huge human and financial costs of war during this century.
- ADV Action Plan: In small teams of four, devise a strategy for making people aware of the large number of small automatic assault weapons that are sold across the world by Russia, the United States, Israel, and South Africa and the tragic effect these weapons are having on the poor of the world. Share your plan with the class.
- ADV Historical Research: Using your school library and the Internet, focus on one small war during the late twentieth century. What caused it? How could it have been prevented? What were its human and financial costs?

7.13.7 The Entropy Trap

An old Chinese saying says it all: "If we do not change direction, we will end up where we are going." Entropy is the process whereby a person, system, or country begins to decline and cannot pull itself out of the decline. It is a scary thought for the planet Earth during the twenty-first century. The economy of the world expanded sixfold between

1950 and 1995 and continues to expand rapidly. The world's total economic output rose a modest 4 percent during 1997. Translated, the 4 percent increase of output was worth approximately $1.1 trillion dollars, or more than the total economic output of the planet during the seventeenth century.

Why should we be worried about entropy when the economy of the world is expanding so fast? The question can be simply stated: Are the individual countries of the world expanding so fast they are outrunning the resources of the planet Earth?

1. The Population Trap (see table 7.13.1): Is the population of planet Earth—increasing at eighty million per year—threatening to out-eat and out-drink the resources of the planet?
2. The Food Trap (see table 7.13.2): Is the total grain production of the planet Earth—while increasing—keeping up with the population growth of the world?
3. The Water Trap (see table 7.13.3): Is the supply of fresh water in some of the most crucial areas of the planet Earth—China, India, Pakistan, North Africa, the Middle East, and southwestern North America—keeping up with increasing food demands for crop irrigation in these areas?
4. The Climate Trap (see table 7.13.4): Is the temperature of the planet Earth—rising for some time—caused by natural causes or human actions? The rapidly increasing economies of the world with their high consumption of fossil fuels contribute a great deal of temperature to the atmosphere. Can we humans afford to wait and find out if our dependence on burning fossil fuels is a cause of the planet's rise in temperature?
5. The Poverty Trap (see table 7.13.5): Is the split between the rich and the poor in the world—with the 20 percent richest people and countries of the world consuming over 80 percent of the world's economic resources—becoming too wide?
6. The War Trap (see 7.13.6): Is the population of planet Earth spending too large of a proportion of the world's economic resources on building weapons of war, waging war, and then rebuilding from the devastating effects of war?

Are these planetary signs indicators of impending decline and entropy for the planet Earth? If so, do we have time to sit and wait until the world collapses around us? Can a shift in the policies of the planet

Earth to a carefully planned project of sustained development take place to reverse virtually all of the indicators of entropy? Major questions to implement such a plan of sustained development might focus on the following (Boulding 1964, 137–155; Brown et al. 1998, 168–187):

1. Can a worldwide emphasis be placed on renewable resources and recycling of steel, paper, water, and garbage?
2. Can the planet shift away from fossil fuels to solar, wind, and hydrogen power sources?
3. Can the planet change its mode of transportation away from cars to more mass transportation and bicycles?
4. Can the planet focus on conserving existing water resources and developing ocean water desalinization systems?
5. Can a strong worldwide effort take place to protect existing cropland from erosion?
6. Can a change take place to shift human consumption from grain-intensive beef and pork to more grain efficient animals, such as poultry?
7. Can a global effort take place to educate the people of the world to stabilize their populations?
8. Can the countries of the planet shift even a small part of their military economies to peacekeeping?

- Quick Write: For a minute, stop and think of something you saw during the past week that was wasteful in your community or school. In a short paragraph, describe this wastefulness and share your thoughts with the class.
- Poster Power: Create an advertising poster to promote sustained development for the planet Earth.
- T Chart: Make a T chart to compare wasteful things you are currently doing at home and school and a second list of how you could improve each of these practices to be less wasteful.
- Quick Skit: With a team of four students, create a short dramatization that illustrates many of the wasteful habits of our planet's people and how they can improve these for sustained development.
- Art Mart: Create a drawing or a painting that illustrates the principle of sustained development.
- Futurist #1: In a poem or rap, create a story of a planet in decline due to the wasteful habits of its people.

- Futurist #2: In a short story, describe how a group of students were able to start a trend for using renewable resources and sustained development on their planet.
- Time Traveler: A time traveler has come back from the future to warn the planet Earth. Create a short skit with a partner that illustrates what warning the time traveler brings to our planet.
- Front Page: With a team of four student editors, create a front-page edition of the *Digital Times* that illustrates some of the major problem the planet Earth faces as it enters the twenty-first century.
- Opinion Poll: Conduct an opinion poll on your school campus, at home, and in your neighborhood with the questions above to see if they are willing to change to a sustainable economy. Pool your findings with the rest of the class to make a report on the possibilities of sustained development during the twenty-first century.
- ADV Research an Action Plan: Using resources in your library and on the Internet, research how different communities have created their own local models of sustained development.
- ADV Implement an Action Plan: As a class, create and implement a schoolwide and local action plan to promote sustained development.

7.14.0   ERA ANTECEDENTS FOR THE FUTURE

7.14.1   Is Humankind Ready to Advance?

It is now time to judge whether or not humankind is ready to advance into the next era:

- Five members from around Digital Town (the class) will state their basic viewpoints of whether or not humankind should move forward. The five illustrious members are as follows:
  1. Neutron Limdunk, the archconservative of Digital Town, who believes that humankind has gone far enough with enough progress. Limdunk believes strongly that the good old days were the best and that humankind needs to hold strongly to past values and beliefs.
  2. Rudy Deru, one of the rising young voices in the town, is a more moderate conservative who believes that we need to be very cautious with any change and be very sure that no harm will come to Digital Town if change takes place. Rudy is willing to accept

some change, but only in very small amounts and only when the time is right—and Rudy wants to decide when that time will come.

3. Willie Wookwam, the wishy-washy middle-of-the-roader around town, is willing to accept change for a few minutes after one speaker, but may have a change of mind in an instant to oppose change after another speaker has finished.

4. Larty Vatsmeer, the moderate progressive of the group is willing to support change for the good of the people in Digital Town. Vatsmeer is especially in favor of change when it will benefit Vatsmeer's own family directly.

5. Garcia Varull, the radical progressive of the town, is very willing to support any change that will move humanity away from a poor basement apartment into something more modern and comfortable for humanity.

- Members of Digital Town (classroom) now must chose one of the five positions for humanity to take and support their position with evidence of what they have learned about the twentieth century.

- A vote will then be taken to determine whether or not humanity should move on to the next era. The consensus decision of the imaginary citizens of Digital Town will determine their own future and the rest of humanity. (In reality, such decisions by people during the twentieth century were key in deciding whether humans stayed the way they were or progressed to new levels of development.)

Full Thematic Table of Contents

Traditional World History: Chronological and Regional Table of Contents

Asia, Africa, America, and the Middle East Twentieth-Century Thematic Lesson Pacs (1900–1999)

Major World Problems at the end of the Twentieth Century— Thematic Lesson Pacs (1900–1999)

Basic Map Resources

Absolutely the best source of maps for any world history class is the CD-ROM by Broderbund entitled Maps N Facts. Any map of any country or continent can be instantly analyzed or printed out for duplication, along with a massive wealth of CIA data on any area of the world. Maps N Facts is available from Broderbund, P.O. Box 6125, Novato, CA 94948. Another excellent source on the Internet is Bruce Jones Designers' World of Maps (see http://www.bjdesign.com) from which you can download excellent sets of maps for both the IBM-PC and MAC computers for a low initial price. (BJDesign is the source for the continental global maps that are contained in this appendix).

The Internet also contains a wealth of other map sources for a wide variety of needs. For example, the Library at the University of Texas-Austin has a large collection of Asian maps available on the Web at www.lib.utexas.edu/PCL/Mapcollection/asia.html. A West End London bookstore, Altea Maps & Books, sells antique maps on-line at www.antique-maps.co.uk. For a comprehensive site of world maps on the Web, The Map Guide! at wwww.algonet.se/~cristar/index.htm lists almost every map available on the Web by continents, countries, and region. Check them out!

Recommended Classroom Background Music by Time Period

Unit 5—Enlightenment Classroom Background Music

The Enlightenment was a glorious era for music. The gracious musical arpeggios of this era paralleled the ornate architectural designs and dress of baroque courts of Europe. A sampling of these magnificent sounds of this baroque period includes the following:

Johann Sebastian Bach, *Brandenburg Concertos* (Philharmonia Slavonia, PMG CD. 160 407).

Antonio Vivaldi, *The Four Seasons* (Musici de San Marco, PMG CD. 160 109).

Wolfgang Amadeus Mozart, *Symphonies 21, 30, and 33* (Mozart Festival Orchestra, PMG CD. 160 114).

Canadian Brass, *High, Bright, Light and Clear—The Glory of Baroque Brass* (CD RCD14574).

A last, great classroom background music addition is the beautiful Spanish baroque composition *Luz y Norte* of 1677 by Spanish composer Ruiz de Ribayaz. This stunning piece of music is recreated in Spanish dances by the Harp Consort under the direction of Andrew Lawrence King (Deutsche Harmonia Mundi CD. 05472-77340-2, available through BMG).

Unit 6—Nineteenth-Century Classroom Background Music

The power and force of the early nineteenth century can be felt especially through Ludwig von Beethoven's Fifth Symphony. There is no better way to listen and study this symphony than through a CD-ROM entitled *Beethoven's 5th—The Multimedia Symphony* (available from Future Vision Multimedia, telephone 1-800-472-8777). Listen to Beethoven's Fifth straight. Project the written music on a screen as the symphony is playing. Analyze Beethoven's composition of this Fifth Symphony section by section. Listen to each instrument in the orchestra separately. This is a magnificent introduction to the master musician of the early nineteenth century.

Although just a CD without the ROM, a feeling of the late nineteenth century can well be heard in Richard Wagner's powerful *Der "Ring" Ohne Worte* (The "Ring" without Words) without the cosmic blasts of Wagner's singers, by Lorin Maazel and the Berliner Philharmoniker (TELARC CD-80154).

Unit 7—Twentieth-Century Classroom
Background Music

A single music idiom did not exist for the twentieth century. The classical music traditions of the nineteenth century continued, but with startling diversity. Dynamically new musical genre emerged during the century—primarily blues, jazz, rock, and their many offshoots. Listed are representative samples of twentieth-century music arranged by decade, which should provide excellent background music to the study of each of these periods:

Claude Debussy (from France, 1900s) *Le Mer, L'Apres* and *Midi d'un Faune*. Leonard Bernstein and the New York Philharmonic. Sony CD. SMK47546.

Jelly Roll Morton (from the United States, 1910s) *Blues & Stomps from Rare Piano Rolls*. Biograph Records. CD B000003HLL.

George Gershwin (from the United States, 1920s) *An American in Paris, Cuban Overture, and Porgy and Bess*. Eduardo Mata and the Dallas Symphony Orchestra. RCA. CD 7726-2-RV.

Benny Goodman (from the United States, 1930s) *Benny Goodman—Live at Carnegie Hall*. Columbia CD. G2K 40244.

Aaron Copland (from the United States, 1940s) *The Copland Collection: Orchestral & Ballet Works 1936–1948*. Sony CD. SM3K 46559.

Elvis Presley (from the United States, 1950s). *Elvis—The King of Rock & Roll: The Complete 50s Masters*. RCA CD. 07863 66050 2.

The Beatles (from England, 1960s). *The Beatles—Past Masters Vol-*

ume One. EMI Records CD. COP 7 90043 2.

Miles Davis (from the United States 1960s). *Kind of Blue*. Columbia CD. CK64935.

Bob Marley (from Jamaica, 1970s). *Bob Marley & The Wailers—Uprising*. Tuff Gong Island Records CD. 422 846 211 2.

Isaac Hayes (from the United States, 1970s). *Isaac Hayes—Greatest Hit Singles*. Stax Records. SCD-8515-2.

Credence Clearwater Revival (from the United States, 1970s). *Credence Clearwater Revival—Chronicle*. Fantasy FCD 623 CCR2.

Madonna (from the United States, 1980s). *The Immaculate Collection*. Warner Brothers CD. B000002LND.

U2 (from Ireland, 1990s). *U2—War*. Island Records. CD 90067-2.

Recommended CD-ROMs and Web Sites by Time Period

Unit 5—Enlightenment CD-ROMs and Web Sites

No one Internet site, to date, exists on the Enlightenment. A good source, however, is the Malaspina Great Books Web site from Malaspina University in Canada at www.mala.bc.ca/~MCNEIL, which provides an excellent base to begin a study of the major authors and thinkers of the Enlightenment, such as Cervantes, Galileo, Descartes, and Bacon. The site also provides direct links for each author to Library of Congress citations and even a link with Amazon.com to buy books directly on-line. Another very good site is the On-Line Data Archive of the eighteenth- and nineteenth-century slave movement at http://dpls.dacc.wisc.edu/slavedata/index.html, which provides a large database of raw data and documentation of such records as the Virginia slave trade during the eighteenth century, the slave trade to Rio de Janeiro, the English slave trade, and the slave trade to Havana, Cuba.

Unit 6—Nineteenth-Century CD-ROMs and Web Sites

As of summer 2001, there is no one site on the Internet focused on the nineteenth century. Many sites, however, can be located on the sites of major individuals who contributed to nineteenth-century society. Examples include the many Web sites on Claude Monet and the history of impressionist paintings. A major site linking these sites is Claude Monet Lien/Links at http://giverny.org/monet/links/index.htm. Authors such as the great Russian writer F. M. Dostoevsky are the focus of a variety of Web sites, including Concordances of the Complete Works of F. M. Dostoevsky at http://www.karelia.ru/~Dostoevsky/dostconc/aboute.htm.

Note, however, that many of these great sources are in the native languages of their authors. A great source for looking for nineteenth-century authors in English translation is the Great Books Index, which has many full texts of authors on-line, such as Karl Marx at http://books.mirror. org/gb.marx.html, for such works as *Capital* or *The Manifesto of the Communist Party* in English or French.

Unit 7—Twentieth-Century CD-ROMs and Web Sites

A wide variety of excellent CD-ROMs exists on the twentieth century. By far the best—and a must for every classroom—is *Our Times—A Multimedia Encyclopedia of the 20th Century* (ViCarious CD ROM VIC025, telephone: 415-610-8300). Microsoft's Encarta CD-ROM 59111 is also a good choice for twentieth-century references. Perhaps the best source available for CD-ROMs on the twentieth century is WAE—History, Military History, and Aviation CD-ROM Catalog at http://wae.com/webcat/webcat.htm, which is a gold mine of CD-ROM titles on the twentieth century, biographies, world history, and gigabytes of clip art and film clips on every conceivable war, weapon, and battle from the Trojan War to Desert Storm. Examples of CD-ROM tiles that can be ordered from WAE include *Great Generals of the 20th Century*, *Seven Days in August* (the construction of the Berlin Wall, 1961), *The Sixties: America 1960–1970*, *The Day after Trinity* (Oppenheimer and the building of the Atomic Bomb), *Gandhi: Apostle of Peace and Nonviolence*, and *Apartheid and the History of the Struggle for Freedom in South Africa*. Any picture or sound of the twentieth century, however, would be incomplete without John Coltrane's *Blue Note* (Blue Note CD-ROM 53428), originally recorded in 1957 but remastered in the 1990s as an amazing visual and auditory record of jazz at midcentury on CD-ROM.

Annotated Bibliography

Ade Ajayi, J. F., and Ian Espie. 1965. *A Thousand Years of West African History*. Ibadan Nigeria: Ibadan University Press.
A classical and masterful source for information on West African history.

Anobile, Richard J. 1971. *Why a Duck?* New York: Darien House.
An absolute riot of visual and oral gems from the Paramount Pictures' Marx Brothers' films of the 1930s. Perhaps the highest point of comedy during the twentieth century.

Aoki, Michiko Y., and Margaret B. Dardess. 1981. *As the Japanese See It— Past and Present*. Honolulu: University Press of Hawaii.
A collection of historical Japanese stories and essays on such themes as religion, society, and politics.

Bailey, Sidney D. 1963. *The United Nations—A Short Political Guide*. New York: Praeger.
A good, short introduction to the United Nations.

Boorstin, Daniel J. 1992. *The Creators: A History of the Heroes of Imagination*. New York: Random.

Bouhler, Philipp. 1938. *Kampf um Deutschland—Ein Lesebuch für die Deutsche Jugend*. Berlin: Zentralverlag der NSDAP.
A Nazi reader for young people (in German) describing the strength of the German people under their leader, Adolf Hitler.

Boulding, Kenneth E. 1964. *The Meaning of the 20th Century: The Great Transition*. New York: Harper Colophon Books.
An excellent short monograph on the problems facing the twentieth century.

Bronowski, J. 1973. *The Ascent of Man*. Boston: Little, Brown.
A beautiful and brilliant history of the human intellect.

Brown, Lester, et al. 1997. *Vital Signs—1997*. Washington, D.C.: World Watch Institute.
An annual powerful book of statistics and graphs on the most critical signs of the health of the planet Earth and its people. Also available on computer disk.

———, ed. 1998a. *State of the World—1998*. Washington, D.C.: World Watch Institute.
The most authoritative source of information on the state of the world each year and translated into most of the world's major languages.

———, et al. 1998b. *World Watch Paper #143: Beyond Malthus—Sixteen Dimensions of the Population Problem*. Washington, D.C.: World Watch Institute.

———, and Jennifer Mitchell. 1998. Building a New Economy. *State of the World—1998*. Washington, D.C.: World Watch Institute.

Burchell, S. C. 1966. *Age of Progress*. New York: Time-Life.
A beautifully illustrated short history of the nineteenth century.

Capra, Fritjof. 1996. *The Web of Life*. New York: Anchor.
A brilliant synthesis of recent thinking tying together the ideas of complexity, Gaia, and chaos theory with explanations of living organisms, ecosystems, and social systems.

Carey, John, ed. 1987. *Eyewitness to History*. New York: Avon.
Perhaps one of the most extensive collections of firsthand historical accounts of major events in world history.

Chang, Iris. 1995. *Thread of the Silkworm*. New York: Basic.
The account of a monumental blunder by the United States during the communist witch hunts of the McCarthy era. Dr. Tsien Hsue-shen—one of the critical pioneers of America's rocketry program—was falsely accused of being a communist and sent back to China where, of course, he founded China's rocketry program.

Collingwood, R. G. 1956. *The Idea of History*. New York: Galaxy.
A classic source on the philosophy of history.

Chambers, E. K. 1930. *William Shakespeare*. Oxford: Oxford University Press.
A classic source on information about the Elizabethan bard.

Davis, Philip J., and Reuben Hersh. 1986. *Descartes' Dream: The World According to Mathematics*. Boston: Houghton Mifflin.
In 1619, Descartes proposed that the world should be seen through the eyes of mathematics. Davis and Hersh present a powerful argument against using Descartes' reasoning.

Dubos, Rene. 1974. *Beast or Angel? Choices That Make Us Human*. New York: Scribner's.
A fundamental book for the beginning of human history focusing on a discussion that should take place at the start of every class in history.

Durant, Will, and Ariel Durant. 1961. *The Age of Reason Begins*. New York: Simon & Schuster.

Ellwood, Robert S., Jr. 1980. *An Invitation to Japanese Civilization*. Belmont, Calif.: Wadsworth.
A short and lively introduction to the social and intellectual history of Japan.

Flavin, Christopher, and Seth Dunn. 1998. Responding to the Threat of Climate Change. *State of the World—1998*. Washington, D.C.: World Watch Institute.

Fletcher, Sir Banister. 1896. *A History of Architecture on the Comparative Method*. London: B. T. Batsford.
A beautiful, old book full of architectural drawings of some of the great buildings of the world.

Foster, John J., and Fred Magdoff. 1998. Liebig, Marx, and the Depletion of Soil Fertility: Relevance for Today's Agriculture. *Monthly Review* 50 (July/August): 32–45.

French, Hilary F. 1998. Assessing Private Capital Flows to Developing Countries. *State of the World—1998*. Washington, D.C.: World Watch Institute.

Gardner, Gary. 1998. Recycling Organic Wastes. *State of the World—1998*. Washington, D.C.: World Watch Institute.

Gay, Peter. 1966. *Age of Enlightenment*. New York: Time-Life.
A beautifully illustrated introduction to the philosophers, rationality, and sentimentality of the Enlightenment.

Gribbin, John. 1984. *In Search of Schrodinger's Cat: Quantum Physics and Reality*. New York: Bantam.
A classic introduction to quantum physics.

Guedj, Denis. 1996. *Numbers: The Universal Language*. New York: Abrams.
A beautiful and very readable history of numbers and mathematics.

Hamilton, Carolyn, ed. 1995. *The Mefacane Aftermath*. Johannesburg, South Africa: Witwatersrand University Press.
A masterpiece of recent research about Shaka and the Difaqane (Mefecane, Defacane) that followed him.

Harper, Ida Husted. 1908/1969. *Life and Work of Susan B. Anthony*. Indianapolis, Ind.: Bowen-Merill.
The definitive work on Susan B. Anthony.

Hawking, Stephen. 1990. *A Brief History of Time from the Big Bang to Black Holes*. New York: Bantam.
A brilliant introduction to the human-created concept of time.

Hochschild, Adam. 1998. *King Leopold's Ghost:—A Story of Greed, Terror, and Heroism in Colonial Africa*. Boston: Houghton Mifflin.

A detailed and important account of the colonial experience in the Congo, which goes a long way to shed the myth of a benevolent Europe spreading civilization with its colonial empires.

Hulme, Peter, and Ludmilla Jordanova. 1990. *The Enlightenment and Its Shadows*. New York: Routledge.
An intellectual collection of essays on the views of nature, music, economics, and politics of the Enlightenment.

Jacobus, Lee A, ed. 1994. *The World of Ideas*. Boston: St. Martin's Press.

Kennedy, Paul. 1987. *The Rise and Fall of the Great Powers*. New York: Random.
A powerful study of the cycles of political states.

Lankevic, George J., and Wallace Sokosky. 1979. *The World and the West: Readings in Contemporary History*. Wayne, N.J.: Avery.
An excellent collection of documents that represent the essential thinking of the nineteenth and twentieth centuries.

Liao, Kuang-Sheng. 1984. *Anti-Foreignism and Modernization in China: 1860–1980*. Hong Kong: Chinese University Press.
An authoritative and in-depth historical analysis of the major forces and traditions that make up modern China today.

Manley, Deborah. 1992. *The Guinness Book of Records—1492*. New York: Facts on File.
Simply one of the most interesting books in print. Each page is full of economic, social, political, and geographic information about the year 1492.

McGinn, Anne Platt. 1988. Promoting Sustainable Fisheries. *State of the World—1998*. Washington, D.C.: World Watch Institute.

McMaster, H. R. 1997. *Dereliction of Duty*. New York: Harper Collins.
A powerful, well-documented tale of how the United States entrapped itself in Vietnam.

McNeil, William H. 1977. *Plagues and People*. New York: Anchor Doubleday.
The classic source for information on the black plague and other epidemics.

Mee, Charles L., Jr. 1993. *Playing God: Seven Fateful Moments When Great Men Met to Change the World*. New York: Simon & Schuster.
An excellent source on the meetings between Attila and Pope Leo I, Cortés and Montezuma, and the meetings at Versailles and Yalta following World Wars I and II.

Meskill, John. 1965. *The Pattern of Chinese History*. Boston: D. C. Heath.
An excellent short source for the major problems confronting Chinese history (for example, cycles, development, or stagnation). One of Heath's series, Problems in Asian Civilizations.

Michael, Franz. 1986. *China through The Ages*. Boulder, Colo.: Westview Press. *An interesting high-level history of the major trends in Chinese history.*

Moynahan, Brian. 1997. *Rasputin: The Saint Who Sinned*. New York: Random. *It is doubtful that a stranger man ever lived. A Russian mystic who had a magical power over the Russian royal family before the Russian Revolution of 1917.*

Nicholl, Charles. 1992. *The Reckoning—The Murder of Christopher Marlowe*. New York: Harcourt, Brace.
A fascinating and real spy/counterspy Elizabethan murder mystery involving a major young English playwright-spy and contemporary of William Shakespeare.

Ninck, C. 1886. *Deutsche Kinderfreund—8 Jahrgang*. Hamburg: Expedition. *A collection of nineteenth-century masterpieces of German iron engravings on nonacidic paper buried inside a children's book, illustrated by A. O. Mener.*

Pahl, Ron H. 1997. Maybe Shakespeare Was Right about "Race"! *Multicultural Education* (spring): 12–17.
An important article on the historical evolution of the word "race" in the English language.

Palmer, Alan. 1974. *Age of Optimism*. Milestones of History, vol. 8. New York: Newsweek Books.
A wonderful visualization of the history of the early nineteenth century, from the Louisiana Purchase to Perry's opening of Japan (1803–1854).

Pearson, Carol S. 1989. *The Hero Within: Archetypes We Live By*. San Francisco: Harper & Row.
A masterpiece of understanding the role myths and archetypes play in shaping the lives of individual humans and nations.

Prange, Gordon W. 1984. *Target Tokyo: The Story of the Sorge Spy Ring*. New York: McGraw Hill.
One of the most overlooked facets of history is the spy. Sorge was one of the master spies and counterspies of World War II who greatly affected the outcome of the war.

Prigogine, Ilya. 1996. *The End of Certainty*. New York: Free Press.
Perhaps one of the most important books of the late twentieth century in understanding the relationship between scientific certainty, the relationship of humanity with the universe, and the direction humanity is taking toward the future.

Renner, Michael. 1994. *World Watch Paper #122: Budgeting for Disarmament: The Costs of War and Peace*. Washington, D.C.: World Watch Institute.
A tight summary of the world's military buildup by one of the leading experts in the world on the topic.

———, 1998. Curbing the Proliferation of Small Arms. *State of the World—1998*. Washington, D.C.: World Watch Institute.
A disturbing depiction of the numbers of small arms available to anyone in the world.

Schiller, Gunther. 1968. *Early Jazz: Its Roots and Musical Development*. New York: Oxford University Press.
A basic source on the origins of jazz.

Scott, Robert Falcon. 1914. *Scott's Last Expedition*. London: Smith, Elder.
The riveting journals of Scott's unsuccessful attempt to reach the South Pole.

Sobel, Dava. 1995. *Longitude: The True Story of a Lone Genius Who Solved the Greatest Scientific Problem of His Time*. New York: Walker.
An exciting history of William Harrison's invention of a portable chronometer to accurately measure the longitude of the Earth during the mid-eighteenth century.

Stambrook, F. G. 1969. *European Nationalism in the Nineteenth Century*. London: Frederick Warne.
An excellent short monograph on the topic.

Stuart, James, and D. McK. Malcolm. 1950. *The Diary of Henry Francis Fynn*. Piertmaritzburg South Africa: Shuter and Shooter.
Fynn's diary is the essential firsthand source on Shaka that documents Fynn's visits with Shaka and the Zulu nation in South Africa between 1824 and 1828.

Sussman, Robert W. 1997. Exploring Our Basic Human Nature: Are Humans Inherently Violent? *Anthro Notes* 19 (fall): 1–6, 17–19.
A great starting point for any thoughtful class on the history of humanity.

Taylor, Bayard. 1861. *Cyclopedia of Modern Travel: A Record of Adventure, Exploration, and Discovery for the Past Sixty Years*, vol. 2. New York: Moore, Wilstach, Keys.
A classic compendium of early nineteenth-century writings and etchings, including Moffat's missionary work in southern Africa, Livingstone's explorations of central Africa, Fremont's explorations of California, Burton's travels to Mecca, and Perry's opening of Japan.

Ulich, Robert. 1971. *Progress or Disaster? From the Bourgeois to the World Civilization*. New York: New York University Press.

Waters, Maurice. 1967. *The United Nations International Organization and Administration*. New York: Macmillan.
Waters is a basic reference to any aspect of the history and organization of the UN.

Watson, Francis. 1974. *A Concise History of India*. London: Hames and Hudson.
A well-written and illustrated history of India from the Aryan invasions to the rule of Indira Gandhi.

Wilton, Andrew. 1979. *J. M. W. Turner—His Art and Life*. Secaucus, N.J.: Poplar.
A large, magnificently illustrated volume of the works of Turner.

Wood, Ellen Meiksins. 1998. The Agrarian Origins of Capitalism. *Monthly Review* 50 (July/August): 14–31.

Zentner, Kurt. 1963. *Illustrierte Geschichte des Zweiten Weltkriegs* (The Illustrated History of the Second World War). Munich: Sudwest Verlag Newmann.
A massive, well-documented history of World War II from the German side, written in German.

About the Author

Ron Pahl is a longtime world history buff who does not like history teachers who bore their students. He has climbed the pyramids of Giza several times, sat with his feet in the reflecting pool of the Taj Mahal, and meditated with monks at Ankhor Wat. Why can't students actively simulate such exciting historical experiences in the classroom? His belief is that students learn more in active, rigorous, and enjoyable classrooms and he has applied this belief to his high school classrooms for more than twenty years. He currently teaches and coordinates the social studies teacher education program at California State University, Fullerton.